COLOR IN SPACE

brightening it up

SendPoints

COLOR IN SPACE
brightening it up

© SendPoints Publishing Co., Ltd.

SendPoints

EDITED & PUBLISHED BY SendPoints Publishing Co., Ltd.
PUBLISHER: Lin Gengli
PUBLISHING DIRECTOR: Lin Shijian
EDITORIAL DIRECTOR: Sundae Li
EXECUTIVE EDITOR: Luka Yu, Christina Hwang
ART DIRECTOR: Lin Shijian
EXECUTIVE ART EDITOR: Wang Xue
PROOFREADING: Sundae Li, Karly Hedley

ADDRESS: Room 15A Block 9 Tsui Chuk Garden, Wong Tai Sin, Kowloon, Hong Kong
TEL: +852-35832323 / **FAX:** +852-35832448
EMAIL: info@sendpoints.cn

DISTRIBUTED BY Guangzhou SendPoints Book Co., Ltd.
SALES MANAGER: Zhang Juan (China), Sissi (International)
GUANGZHOU: +86-20-89095121
BEIJING: +86-10-84139071
SHANGHAI: +86-21-63523469
EMAIL: overseas01@sendpoints.cn
WEBSITE: www.sendpoints.cn

ISBN 978-988-12944-9-4

Artistic Colors

Functional Colors

The Heroism of Color

By Sharon Exley, MAAE, Partner, Architecture Is Fun, Inc.
& Winner of the HUE Color in Architecture Award

Color is essential to our everyday lives. Color is stimulating and soothing, thrilling and expectant, cultural and magical. In our man-made explorations in the spaces in which we work, play, learn, and live, color is part of our everyday lives. While there are countless scholarly treatises on color harmony, color theory, color relativity and psychology, the heroism of color in architecture has been an oft-neglected aspect in design. The projects punctuating these pages are an exception; they demonstrate the visible and tangible influence of color in architecture as a major force and design consideration.

Global authorities on color influence fashion, trend, and design. They provide us with colors of the year and dial-up hues. Understanding how colors can be used and interpreting color forecasts supports the art of color: how color and light are form-givers to architecture, how color enhances context and environment, and how it can communicate a building's sense of purpose.

Architects and designers work with color as part of their art and craft. They personalize selections that balance the left-brained intellectual approach of color theory and harmony with right-brained principles that feel emotive, symbolic, and appropriate. In *Color in Space*, color delivers both architectural and emotional intention. The architects and designers featured celebrate and innovate by using color. Moving through the Toledo Metro Station in Napoli, Italy, commuters now have reasons to linger. Oscar Tusquets Blanca captures and commands their attention with a blue mosaic starry sky, expanding our universe and our perceptions of the underground. The PKO Bank Polski designed by Robert Majkut Design uses a minimal palette of gold, black, and white as a means to ennoble and distinguish private banking experience. Multi-colored metal and translucent tinted glass bands unify the various elements of the Gethsemane Lutheran Church, designed by Olson Kundig Architects, where cross-like forms become a beacon of light and hope, visible inside and out. Strolling under

Summer Umbrella in Portugal is an uplifting dynamic experience; its polychromatic umbrellas bring Mary Poppins-like delight to an urban streetscape. Alejandro Muñoz Miranda's kindergarten in El Chaparral, Granada, Spain uses a rainbow of light to transform a simple form and façade to express a community's care for children. Within the pages of *Color in Space*, color is used symbolically, culturally, and psychologically to define and articulate connections to artful expression.

Artists, designers, and architects all have favorite colors. We use color creatively. We flout convention. Sometimes, our taste in color is idiosyncratic or we follow the norm. We create color combinations that are beautiful in their context. Color is a visual language, conveying the full spectrum of moods and emotions, from strength and solidity to softness and serenity. Color can be symbol and status, magic and memory. Color can connect and create continuity between design elements, and attract, establishing emphasis.

Color is heroic, regardless of typology, size or scale. Choosing to use color as an influence in architecture and design makes its own bold statement. It is brave to design with color. Color makes everyday life brighter, lighter, memorable, and filled with meaning. For the architects and designers within these pages, color is a means of creative exploration and expression, from the exuberant to the emotive. The palette is as limitless as the imagination.

About Architecture Is Fun

Peter J. Exley, FAIA and Sharon Exley, MAAE, Associate ASID, founded the award-winning firm Architecture Is Fun in 1994 focusing on the design of substantive and relevant environments for learning and play through architecture, interiors, exhibits and interpretive experiences, creating places for collaboration and participation that is indispensible for growth and creative development.

Sharon Exley

SUMMER UMBRELLA

ÁGUEDA, PORTUGAL

Words by The Council of Águeda

Águeda is a mid-sized city in Portugal municipality with a total area of 335.3 square kilometers and a total population of more than 50,000. It is situated in a privileged position, between the sea and land, serviced by railroads and expanding road networks. These advantages have allowed the economic and social development of the region, placing Águeda in an important position.

The council of Águeda decided to create an installation to broaden the area's entertainment scope and to further stimulate the development of this ancient cultural city in the annual Agit Águeda event. This summer umbrella street conceived by the council of Águeda, started with the idea of "lift the dark clouds hovering over traditional shops." The local council created this umbrella installation in the trend of urban art with bright colors, hanging above the whole street, making it an inviting place to wander and shop.

Horst Gläsker

www.horst-glaesker.de

The "Bird of Paradise" with the colorful feather head-dress, as Horst Gläsker likes to portray himself, was born in Herford in 1949, studied at the Kunstakademie in Düsseldorf, had his first solo exhibition in the Von der Heydt Museum as early as 1980-81, has held various visiting professorships in Münster and Braunschweig since 1988, and has been a full-time professor at the Kunsthochschule in Kassel since 1998. For a long time he has concerned himself with the dialogue with architecture; he has also created small and large multi-colored sculptures. His approach using words on the steps in Wuppertal, which he himself has walked on many occasions, is of special concern to him and he executes it in a masterly fashion.

SCALA IN WUPPERTAL, GERMANY

Words by Sabine Fehlemann

Not to be confused with La Scala in Milan, Wuppertal in Germany now has its own Scala thanks to Horst Gläsker who, along with his wife Margret Masuch, installed a piece of art into the city by dividing a seemingly average stairway into words relating to relationships.

"Scala" is the Italian word for "steps", Gläsker originally named this installation "Steps of Feelings" or "Scala dei sentimenti."

Sandwiched between houses, each of the 112 steps has been painted a beautiful vibrant colour and labeled with a single word, to escort the climber step by step to the top. Gläsker created this work to make people aware of their feelings, challenge their emotions and encourage people to live in the moment. The steps extend upwards, albeit hardly noticeably, between Gathe and Holsteiner Straße. There are nine landings on the way up, which the artist has employed like paragraph breaks for his word arrangements. In this way, he has formed nine ensembles of words, using adjectives, verbs and nouns, nine sets of steps to recall the different stages of life.

The first four flights each contain 15 steps, in accordance with local building regulations for public spaces which allow no more than 15. Thereafter there are 11 steps on the 5th and 9th flights and between these, 10 steps each.

The first flight represents HOME; here the words refer to family, which **warms**, **protects**, **strokes**, and **caresses**, but can also **terrify** and then go back to **forgive** again. The words in this section speak of **mother** and **happiness**, **home**, **family**, **honor** and **innocence**, but also of **fear** and **remorse**. One can dream up and imagine an entire novel from these simple words.

The second flight could be entitled FRIENDSHIP. Here there are not only nouns and verbs such as **laugh**, **speak**, and **reassure**, which are fitting for this context, but also negatively-tinted words as **arm** and **defend**. Adjectives such as **peaceful** and **aggressive** have been slotted in but it is the nouns which bring it all together with **honesty**, **closeness**, **brother**, **enthusiasm** and **anger**.

Once you arrive at the third flight of steps, CAUTION is called for. Here one walks over such terms as **rage**, **envy**, **accusations**, **trauma**, **lies** and **threat**, which are countered by words such as **respect**, **prudence** and **restraint**.

The fourth flight introduces an unreservedly POSITIVE FEELING—**love**, **affection**, **kiss on the hand**; **passion** and **admirer** are the only nouns. These are joined by adjectives such as **ebullient** and **attractive**, before the verbs make everything clear with **come together**, **seduce**, **yearn**, **fall in love**, **dance** and **tingle**.

The fifth flight shows RESENTMENT, such a powerful emotion summed up in only 11 words this time. **Jealousy**, **panic** and **doubt** are coupled with **rashness**, **lovesickness**, **offence**, **hatred** and **disappointment**. Only three accompanying and explanatory terms remain—**desperate**, **cry** and **feel abandoned**.

The sixth flight re-establishes EQUILIBRIUM in the person striving upwards with a wealth of words in ten parts. It highlights **worth**, **loyalty**, **benevolence**, **depth**, **clarification** and **perseverance**. It advocates **remaining steadfast**, **standing by someone** and **overcoming**.

In the seventh flight, DANGER follows. Here one needs only to go through the list to understand what this is about—**guilt**, **tears**, **vengeance**, **sorrow**, **delusion**, **silence**, **abuse**, **persecution**, **fright** and **terror**. There are only nouns used here.

The great RECONCILIATION lies upon the eighth section. It is based on **hope**, **trust** and **esteem**, **understanding**, **reflection**, **insight** and **sympathy**. Only two verbs are used here to assist—**heal** and **shame**.

The ninth and final flight has now led the exhausted wanderer to the top; here lies SUBLIMITY with **courage**, **sense**, **honor** and **respect**. Now they can enjoy the view in its entirety and the tranquility of freedom. They can now literally look back and consider how much they have achieved by climbing all 112 steps, to be proud and have belief in themselves. The artist shows us, in part with conscious irony, in part seriously, what a long flight of steps can provoke in a climber if he does not just walk over them without thinking.

Gläsker has created minimalist notions here. It has been inspired by Concept Art—he has only preserved the colorfulness. No complete sentences are formed, as with Jenny Holzer (an American conceptual artist); instead, precise words set off a poetic logic. Horst Gläsker was predestined to create such an artistic project, even though this work casts new light on his interests. He does not want to create art for the ghetto, museum or gallery, but integrate art into the everyday environment or, as here, install it into the city architecture.

Wuppertal's steps are an architectonic jewel and a special feature of the city, which since the 19th century has helped to connect the residential districts. The considerable differences in ground elevation led to 469 flights of steps with a total of 12,383 individual steps built. The most famous flight of steps has the very onomatopoeic name of "Tippen-Tappen-Tönchen"—from the sounds produced by visitors when they walk on them. Horst Gläsker has now revealed that steps are not only a way to get from A to B but that they can arouse sensations, and accompany one on a fabulous, verbal journey upwards.

Thanks to Horst Gläsker, these steps, which have long been neglected, now finally begin to tell a story and adjust to the people who walk over them—some walk over pensively; others test themselves physically; some others are occupied with completely different things. Arrays of people find themselves here—families, neighbors, lovers, the troubled, the burdened, loners, even bad people but what these steps can achieve is allowing each person to walk over and look inside.

Artists, who can not only think outside the box to capture people's attention, but use it for social good, have exhibited steady resourcefulness as well as creativity. Incidentally, the font used in this project is called "Humanist".

Artistic Colors

Functional Colors

Artistic Colors

DIDDEN VILLAGE
in Rotterdam, the Netherlands

Designed by MVRDV
Photo© Rob 't Hart

In keeping with MVRDV's ideas about densification over the last 20 years, the first realized
building in its hometown of Rotterdam is a rooftop house extension.

On top of an existing historic house and atelier, bedrooms are positioned as separate volumes, creating privacy for every member of the family. The houses are distributed in such a way that a series of plazas, streets and alleys are caused and increase the feeling of a village on top of a building. Parapet walls with windows surround the new village. Trees, tables, open-air showers and benches are added, optimizing the rooftop lifestyle.

By finishing all elements with a blue polyurethane coating, a new "heaven" is formed. It creates a crown on top of the house. The addition can be seen as a roof life added to the city, a prototype for the further densification of the existing historical area. It explores the costs for beams, infrastructure, and extra finishes, and ultimately aims to be lower in cost than the price of an equivalent ground building.

MORANGIS RETIREMENT HOME
in Paris, France

Designed by Vous Êtes Ici Architectes
Photo© 11H45

French studio Vous Êtes Ici Architectes completed a retirement home in the southern Parisian suburb of Morangis. The building is wrapped with a timber façade while the doors, windows and recesses are picked out in yellow ochre.

The Morangis Retirement Home is divided into three wings within a Y-shaped floorplan. Vous Êtes Ici Architectes arranged the Siberian larch in vertical strips over the façade of the building to form canopies across the three entrances. The main entrance that leads into the center of the building is located at the junction of two wings. Other entry points are positioned along the northern façade for service access, and the southern façade for private resident's gardens.

The building houses four floors that provide functional and administrational areas. Communal rooms, health facilities and staff areas have been grouped together on the first floor. Shared dining rooms, living rooms and other social areas are arranged around the southern elevation and open onto the private resident's garden. The three upper floors of the building are taken up by bedrooms. The areas on the second and third floor accommodate typical residents and are divided into clusters of 13 bedrooms with built-in dining and activity rooms. The fourth floor is dedicated to patients suffering from Alzheimer's and other neurological diseases. Central corridors provide access between different sections of each floor. The designer has also planned two roof terraces with direct access to ground level via a pair of outdoor staircases.

In addition to artificial lighting, large windows have been introduced to allow natural light to filter into the interior helping to provide a fresh atmosphere and create an open space for the residents.

TING 1
In Örnsköldsvik, Sweden

Designed by Wingårdh Arkitektkontor AB thru Gert Wingårdh
Photo© Tord-Rikard

The basis of this colorful addition is the result of an architecture competition in 1961, a concrete court house built by a group of unknown wining architects. Niklas, son of a painter, a local builder bought it with the intention of constructing a tall apartment building on top of the exposed bedrock visible in the atrium. It struck designers immediately that the contrast between the raw concrete of the courthouse and a colorful, maybe even glossy addition might sing.

The team drew up a basically square floor plan, which was then divided into smaller units like hashtags. The layout has five apartments wrapped around this central core, with balconies in all four directions. There are ten similar but varied stories crowned by a rooftop villa for Niklas. The color scheme is based on the art of Bengt Lindström which is Niklas' favourite and is executed in glazed ceramic tiles.

WANANGKURA STADIUM
in Port Hedland, Australia

Designed by ARM Architecture
Photo© Peter Bennetts

Wanangkura Stadium is Port Hedland's new multi-purpose recreational centre. The project includes a new 4,500-square-meter multi-purpose recreation center, with outdoor courts, a landscaped park and external spaces, located at the Kevin Scott Oval site in South Hedland. The building houses a main hall space, short-term child minding facility, gym and fitness rooms, two squash courts and associated seating areas, reception and administration areas, kiosk and tea room facilities, amenities, etc. The structural systems are especially adapted to the local cyclone conditions, the extreme temperatures during summers and the mining industry landscape in the area.

The team's approach to the design considered this building as a mirage—a shimmering, rippling effect on an otherwise flat landscape. Using a "halftone" pixelated technique, the building's entry facade acts as a clear visual image from a long distance, whilst being highly agitated on closer inspection. The opposite side accommodates related facilities, including a spectator's stand, changing rooms and spectator suites.

18 HOMES, STORAGE ROOMS AND A GARAGE
in Madrid, Spain

Designed by RAFAEL CAÑIZARES TORQUEMADA
Photo© RAFAEL CAÑIZARES TORQUEMADA

This project creates a single volume cuboid, aligning with the corner of the plot. It has been designed with modulated façades made of colorful panels, all measuring 225 x 74cm. These walls have resulted from aluminum and fire-proof mineral core colors, highly influenced by the "pixelated" paintings of Paul Klee. Holes of the same size are depressed in the walls at random points. The sliding aluminum powder-coated windows have been given a blue colored face. Sixteen colors weaving together form a multi-colored tapestry, timeless and pleasing to the eyes, far exceeding what the materials simply add up to.

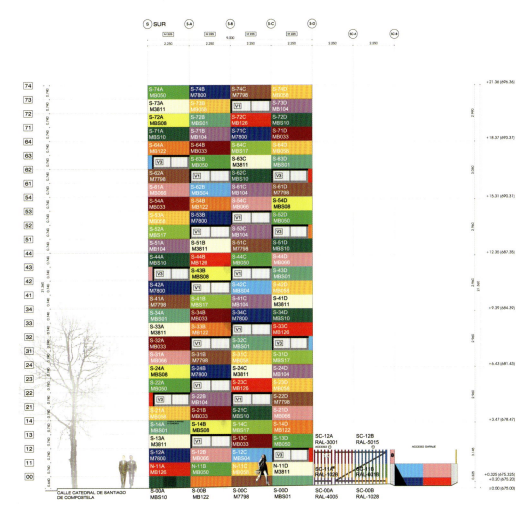

The building manages to bring a parking space, storage room, garage and several homes all under the same roof. The garage ramp is defined as an access to the building, almost sliding down into the building from the sidewalk. It is also decorated with colored panels of the same specification. Within this compact space, almost all of the homes have bedrooms housing at least two windows.

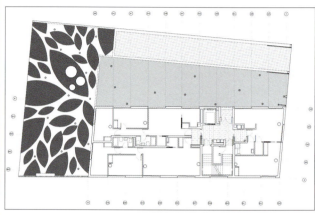

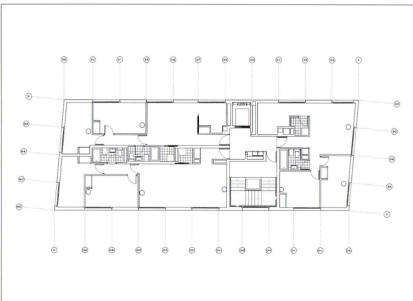

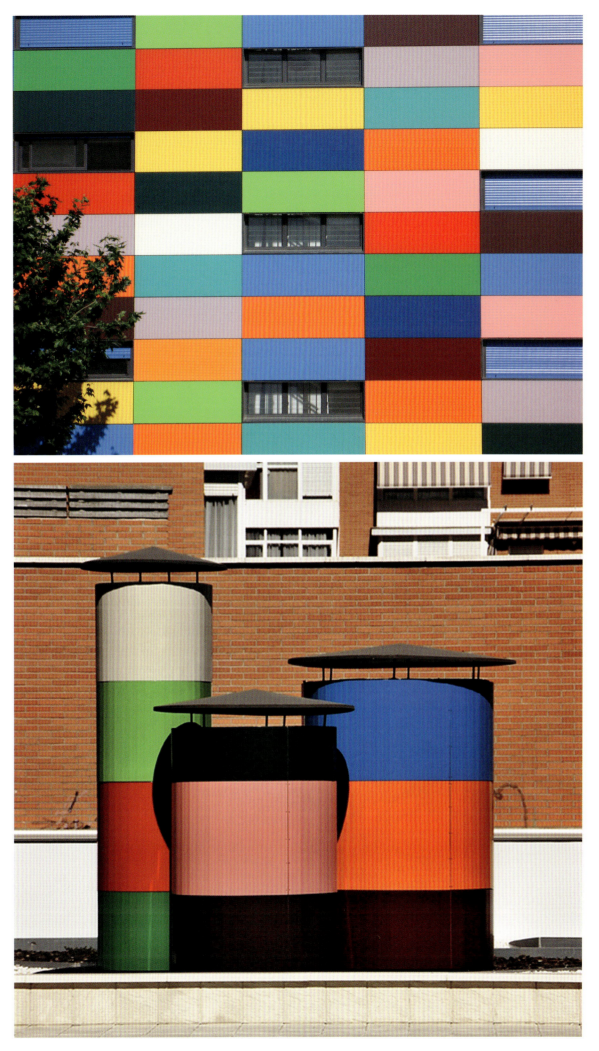

SPORTS HALL "DE RIETLANDEN"
in Lelystad, the Netherlands

Designed by Jetske Bömer, Erik Slangen
Photo© Marcel van der Burg

The new sports hall "De Rietlanden" is sandwiched between two existing sports halls, creating one big sports complex with a spectator stand and a restaurant, servicing both sides on the first floor. Since the location itself was very grey and pale looking, the narrow insert is accentuated by a bright-coloured façade facing the neighbouring buildings. The neon-bright color pallet shows a gradient from green/yellow to blue, which responds to the direct surroundings of green fields and trees on one side, and a blue school building on the other.

Pantone specialty colour PMS codes involved are as follows: Grey White Pantone 420, Bright Green Pantone 389C, Apple Green Pantone 376C, Light Blue Pantone 331C, Blue Pantone 297C, and Yellow Pantone Yellow C.

SUGAMO SHINKIN BANK TOKIWADAI BRANCH
in Tokyo, Japan

Designed by emmanuelle moureaux architecture + design
Photo© Daisuke Shima/ Nacasa & Partners Inc.

Sugamo Shinkin Bank is a credit union that strives to provide first-rate hospitality to its customers in accordance with its motto of "we take pleasure in serving happy customers." This joyful three-story Tokiwadai branch of the bank has been realized by the French-born Japan-based architect and designer Emmanuelle Moureaux. Featuring a distinctive white façade punctured by numerous, variously-sized windows and incorporating a reoccurring theme of leaf motifs, the building aims to give the visiting clients "a natural, rejuvenating feeling".

Upon entering the building, ATMs and teller windows are placed along walls painted with brightly colored leaves on the first floor. The second floor houses the loan section, reception rooms and offices. The third floor is reserved for staff facilities, including changing rooms and a cafeteria. There are seven light-filled "courtyards" housing trees and plants arranged to bring nature into the building.

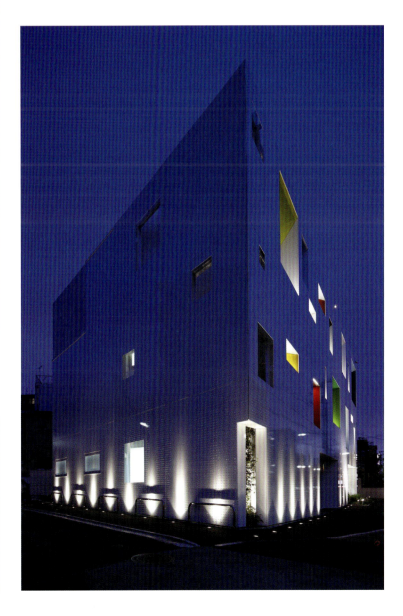

A constellation of leaves in 24 different colors growing on the white branches of the walls and glass windows overlaps with the natural foliage in the courtyards, creating the sensation of being in a magical forest.

THE NURSERY IN LA PAÑOLETA

in Camas, Spain

Designed by Antonio Blanco Montero
Photo© Fernando Alda

Located on the margin of a development area in La Pañoleta, this is the first nursery for families living in social housing and inexpensive accommodations. To achieve the construction of the nursery in a short time frame, it was decided to adopt prefabricated large format building systems: precast concrete panel façades, plasterboard partitions and zinc roofing. Using these together with a steel structure and composite floor slabs has helped to cut the execution time enormously.

The building is designed in an elongated rectangular shape, with courtyards encompassing the whole space of the building. The interior is enveloped in white walls contrasting with yellow aluminum framed windows which act as linear elements that define the wall's white edges. Colored panels of glass in the skylights provide a relaxing atmosphere throughout the building.

The internal partitions between the classrooms can be slid down to the left side of the rooms to form a unique undivided space, which can then be utilized for community activities during holidays.

The colors used here not only represent the vivid image of a nursery, but also make the building an immediate focal point in serving the community as a pre-school education facility. It is one of a kind and keeps sending shockwaves through this developing area.

GETHSEMANE LUTHERAN CHURCH
in Washington, USA

Designed by Olson Kundig Architects
Photo© Matt Anderson

Gethsemane Lutheran Church social services and housing project in Seattle, US was designed by the international firm Olson Kundig Architects within an existing 1950s building. The design for this richly complex project enhances the church's presence in downtown Seattle.

Jim Olson, founding principal of Olson Kundig Architects, led the redmodeling of the building's exterior and the church's main sanctuary, as well as designing the parish life center, a garden and a chapel. In addition to this, Olson has been in collaboration with the project's executive architects SMR to design the five-story affordable housing complex, known as "the hope center".

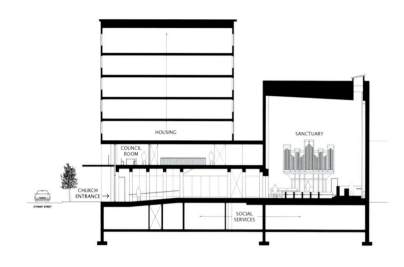

SECTION THROUGH MAIN ENTRY

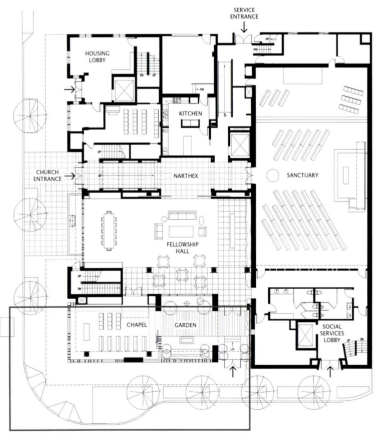

GROUND LEVEL FLOOR PLAN

SECOND LEVEL FLOOR PLAN

Multi-colored metal and glass bands weave the varied segments into a single visual tapestry. From a distance, the gold-finished metal sections interlaced seem to create oversized cross forms. Up close to the building, the warm-toned, handcrafted glass windows of the chapel cast an intimate natural light onto the street, which creates a beacon of light in the city.

A small meditation garden adjoins the chapel and the fellowship hall, balancing openness with outreach. Near the entrance to the church, a statue of Christ stands in a small garden creating a "sidewalk chapel" for passersby.

THE EDUCATIONAL CENTER
in Granada, Spain

Designed by Alejandro Muñoz Miranda
Photo© Javier Callejas

This kindergarten in El Chaparral, a district of Albolote that emerged in the 1950s as a colonization village, was conceived by Spanish architect Alejandro Muñoz Miranda; it has been designed particularly for children up to the age of three years.

This educational center oriented east-west with the main entrance located north is built around a central courtyard onto which all the classrooms open. The courtyard playground links the classrooms and the interior circulation with the garden. The administrative section of the center such as the kitchen and dining areas, the administration area and a gym takes up the greater part of the eastern section, whilst the south is occupied by a long corridor giving access to the classrooms.

The corridors are scattered with multicolored light due to the positioning of the plot and the colored windows, which project the sunlight into the interior. Windows of the classrooms facing north however are plain and much larger, allowing an interesting perspective between the two sections where there is continually changing light. The spatial organization is determined by compression and decompression of the wall and ceiling sections, allowing sections to become smaller or larger, wider or taller. The classrooms are differentiated by age groups, typical of most education centres; however, with their movable partitions they can all be connected to form a whole space for larger group activities. These partitions even when in place permit a visual continuity through their glazed upper sections.

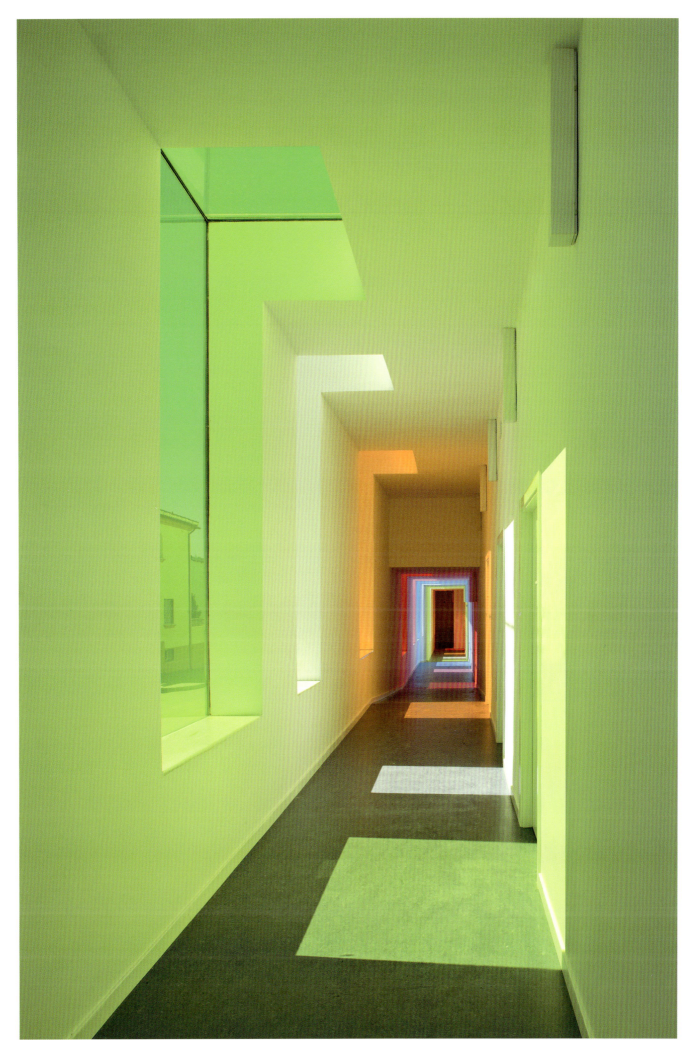

THE SOCIO-CULTURAL CENTER
in Mulhouse, France

Designed by Paul Le Quernec
Photo© 11h45

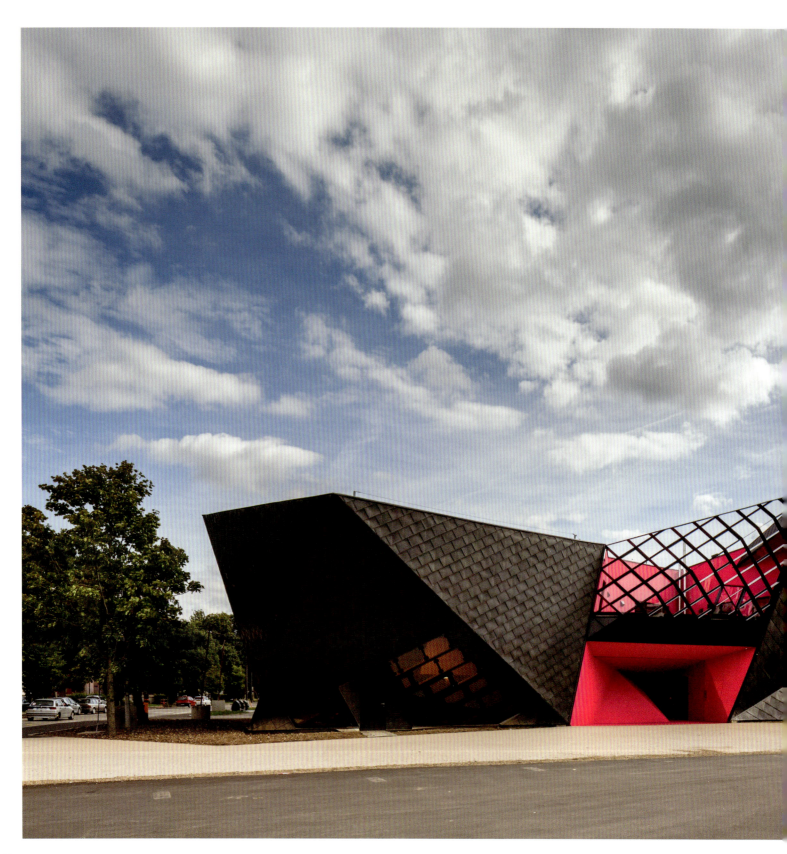

French architect Paul Le Quernec has realized a cultural center in the disadvantaged area of Mulhouse, on a tight plot where structures such as apartments, a public square, a park, children's play areas and other programs have already been predetermined for the rest of the site. Preventing the building from becoming a monolithic block between apartments, Quernec gave triangular geometrics to the building's form, creating a new cultural hub to represent the re-development of the socio-cultural area.

The multi-faceted building's angled lines offer a dynamic structure within this traditional rural town. The central part of the façade is vibrantly coated in magenta, which carries over the height of the two-story section.

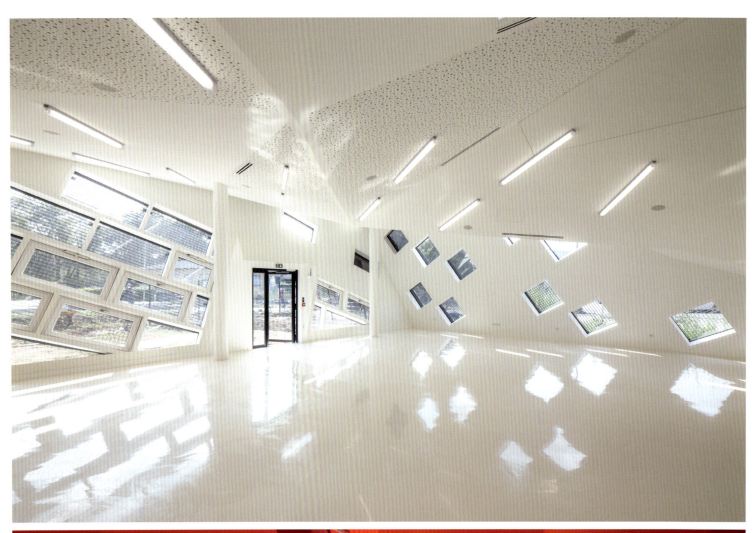

The structure is punctuated by square apertures on its exterior that open up sight lines to provide points of reference from both inside and outside the building. These windows also serve as high-quality illumination on the interior. The first floor is made up of two parts which can be made to work together or separately. They are aligned with one another along the edge of the plot, twisting upwards to the second floor. A small changing room, a teaching kitchen, desks and a box office have been added to allow the space to function as a community hall. On the upper level, a walk-out patio that is protected by a monumental grid overlooks the main piazza in front.

THE SHED
in London, UK
· ·

Designed by Haworth Tompkins
Photo© Helene Binet, Philip Vile

London-based architects Haworth Tompkins have created this temporary venue for the National Theater on London's South Bank. The artistic program pushes creative boundaries, giving the Theater the opportunity to explore new ways of making theater. In the same way, The Shed has also been an experiment by the design team.

The building occupies the previous square, at the front of the National Theater beside the river. Its simple form houses a 225-seat auditorium made of raw steel and plywood. The rough sawn timber cladding refers to the National Theater's iconic board-marked concrete, and the modeling of the auditorium and its corner towers complement the bold geometrics of the Theater itself. A temporary foyer has been carved out from beneath the theater's main external terrace to provide an easy access to the existing foyer.

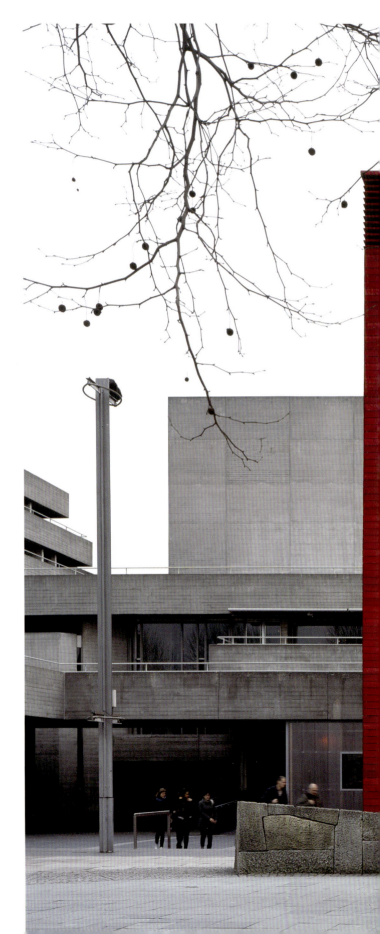

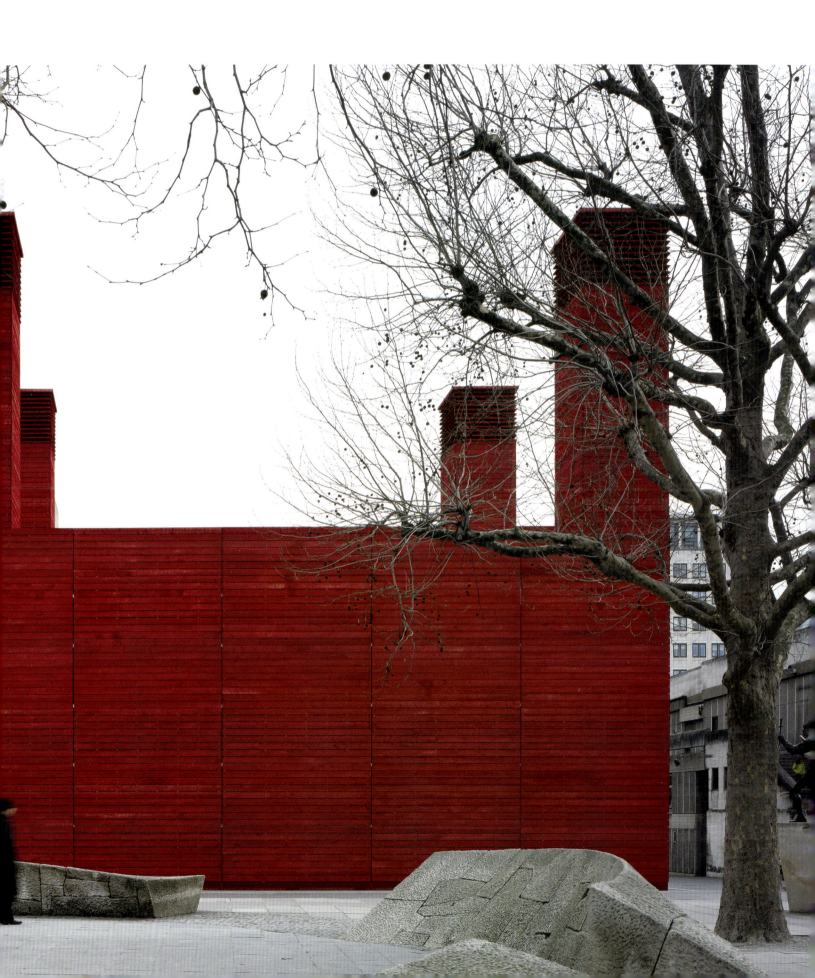

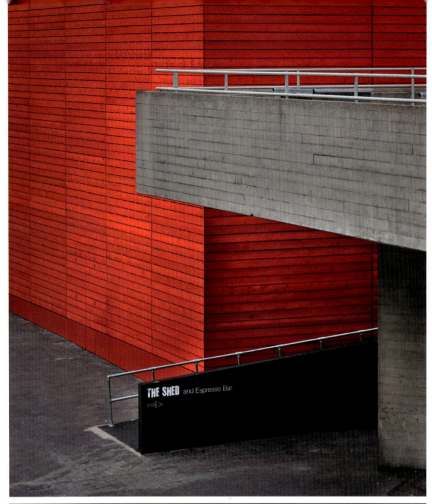

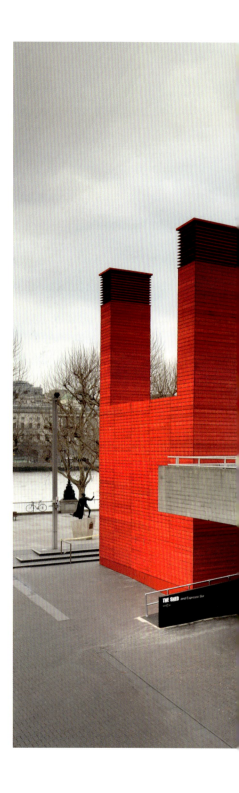

The Shed also represents another step in Haworth Tompkins' ongoing project to research sustainable ways of making theaters, built solely of materials that can be 100% recycled and fitted out with re-used seating. The complex is naturally ventilated, with four towers that draw air through the building providing its distinctive form.

Its temporary nature, built on Haworth Tompkins' earlier temporary projects like the Almeida Theater at Gainsborough Studios and that at King's Cross, permits a structure that can be seen less as a building than as an event or installation—a vibrant intervention on London's South Bank entrance, and sometimes bewilder passers-by.

The Shed's brilliant red color covering the entire mass—without doors or windows, announces its arrival boldly against the geometric, concrete forms of the National Theater, giving it a startling and enigmatic presence.

NESTLE INNOVATION LAB
in Queretaro, Mexico

Designed by rojkind arquitectos
Photo© rojkind arquitectos, by Paul Rivera

In his *Atlantida de hormigón*, Reyner Banham posits "a casual connection, conscious and cultural, between modern architecture and industrial utilitarian structures of an industrial epoch". From Loos and Berhens to Gropius and Le Corbusier among others, in the beginning of the 20th century, a constant back and forth was established between architecture and industrial construction, up until this time marginalized—that would continue to be a characteristic of contemporary architecture. To reinvent the industrial world was a task with which architecture had paid back the favor of having been shown the path as to how to disengage of the heavy formal and stylistical weight of almost two centuries of vacuous rhetoric and ecclesiastic academicism. To reinvent, is understood, as the invention of an image which moves between the operative logic and the logotype.

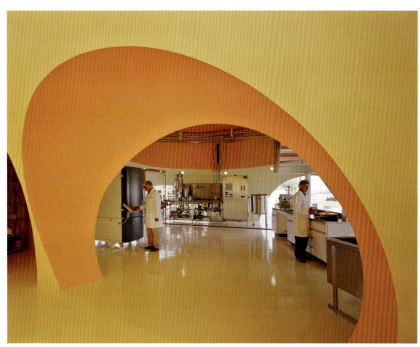

Between this lies what Rojkind arquitectos have done for a pair of factory additions for the Nestlé Company. This commission presented an additional challenge besides its relationship with the existing facility. The UNESCO's designation of Queretaro's historic city center as a world heritage site in 1996, had unforeseen consequences that even expanded to the city's industrial periphery. As a result of this designation, the new building was to have an arched porch, as rooted in tradition. Rojkind responded to this challenge with a reinterpretation not only of the arch but also of the porch. If the arch is nothing else than a fragment of a cupola, in the same vein the cupola is an amplified arch when it rotates around its own axis— the cupola meets the reference criteria of the arch without turning it into a cliché. In this case, a series of spheres intersect and multiply like foam, forming the origin of a continuous open space—a portico. This space expands while another one, made of orthogonal boxes clad in satin mirrored glass, restrains the proliferation of the spheres and houses the specific program requirements for the lab. While the exterior is opaque, metallic and impenetrable in appearance, the interiors of these boxes painted in different colors, have an almost theatrical quality to them: it appears as if the researchers wearing their white robes were floating in a continuous flow of blues, yellows or greens which are interrupted by the continuous spaces of a different color sometimes. When the metal panels that cover the boxes reveal themselves and open like windows, they can be seen from outside.

The construction of the building (if built in a different latitude, a more sophisticated technology most likely would have had been employed to automatize the production of the unique geometries of these spheres) implied that spatial forms was to be realized in a different constructive manner, in a simple almost colloquial way, which allowed local workers to fabricate the foam from spherical cupolas made of rebar rings and arches.

The final result is a series of contrasts that have been unified with apparent simplicity: the exterior metallic, slightly reflective satin color lightly contrasts with and against the bright satin colors of the interiors; the sloped, abstracted planes of the boxes contrast against the exuberance of the interweaving spheres. The strength of this project might be attributed to this game of contrasting opposites, which in a dynamic and changing way depending on the physical view of the observer, can be a dominant characteristic in a moment or a discrete one in another. A rethought and recharged industrial construction thus regains an understanding of what at one time it offered to Architecture: clarity and force.

CASA DAS ARTES
in Miranda do Corvo, Portugal

Designed by FAT
Photo© João Morgado

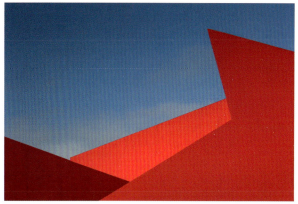

Casa das Artes ("House of the Arts") in Miranda do Corvo expresses the encounter between rural and urban landscapes marked by the Lousã Mountains. The building features a contemporary and volumetrically impressive design. The sloping roofs establish a dialogue with the geometry of the mountain landscape, similar to the village rooftops. The dynamism achieved through the continuity between façades and the roof is accented by a strong red color, emphasizing its design and highlighting the building from the surrounding landscaped area.

More than a building, Casa das Artes is an iconic landmark, celebrating the place where people meet, where culture and art happens, a space capable of promoting and stimulating creative activity, increasing life quality of the people in the area.

The project was conceived by creating versatile spaces, suitable for an array of events, in order to serve the needs of everybody in the community. The outdoor area was optimized to favor landscaped spaces, allowing the creation of an amphitheater for outdoor events, integrated in a garden which is a public space for the village, with several spaces and inviting pathways for leisure.

The building consists of three volumes reflecting different sorts of use: the first one containing the stage areas, the second comprising audience seating and the foyer, and the third with a cafeteria and future museum area, which constitutes a visually independent volume.

The proposed diversity of acess to the building attempts to emphasize the characterization of this site as a public space, allowing the public direct access of specific places, such as the museum area and cafeteria, without passing through the auditorium. The main entrance is through the foyer, which may function as an exhibition area which can also be divided into two by a short flight of stairs. From here depart two paths to an auditorium for nearly 300 people, with a motorized orchestra pit and six levels, properly equipped for holding theater performances, operas, concerts, conferences or lectures. The cafeteria can operate independently from the rest of the building, or even serve as an entrance point to the auditorium. This space has a covered terrace with a skylight oriented west, channeling the sunset into the interior.

SUGAMO SHINKIN BANK SHIMURA BRANCH

in Tokyo, Japan

Designed by emmanuelle moureaux architecture + design
Photo© Daisuke Shima/ Nacasa & Partners Inc.

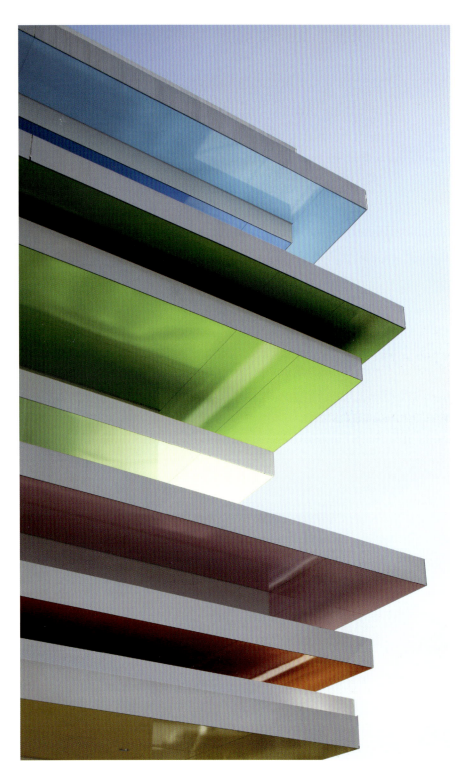

"Color is the theme of all my works. With the concept of 'shikiri', which means dividing space by using colors, I try to introduce modern architecture and traditional elements by creating 3D effects to entice people's different emotions."

With the concept of "Rainbow Millefeuille", the façade of this credit union Sugamo Shinkin Bank Shimura Branch is with a rainbow-like stack of colored layers. Emmanuelle Moureaux created a refreshing atmosphere with a palpable sense of nature based on an open sky motif. Reflected onto the white surface, these colors leave a faint trace, creating a warm and gentle feeling. At night, the colored layers are faintly illuminated. The illumination varies according to the season and time of the day, conjuring up myriads of landscapes.

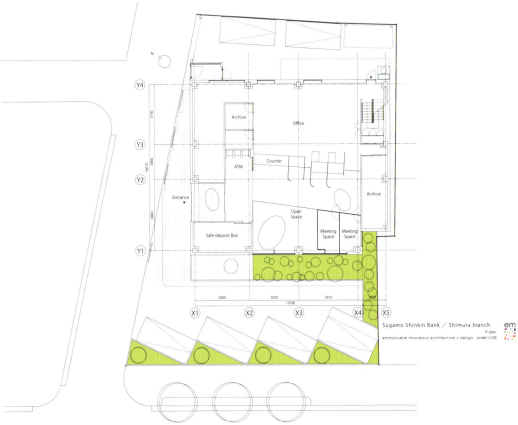

Sugamo Shinkin Bank / Shimura branch
1F plan
emmanuelle moureaux architecture + design   scale:1/100

Upon entering the building, three elliptical skylights bathe the interior in a soft light. Visitors spontaneously look up to see a cut-out piece on the roof that invites them to gaze languidly at it. The ceiling is adorned with dandelion puff motifs that seem to float and drift through the air.

The concept "Shikiri" was inspired by the traditional Japanese "shōji". In traditional Japanese architecture, a shōji is a door, window or room divider, made of translucent paper over a frame of wood which holds together a lattice of wood or bamboo. Shōji may be made of paper such as washi (a style of paper that was first made in Japan) made by modern manufacturing processes. Shōji doors are often designed to slide open, and thus conserve space that would be required by a swinging door. They are used in traditional houses as well as Western-style housing, especially in "washitsu" (Japanese-style room). But in modern construction, shōji does not form the exterior surface of a building; it sits inside a sliding glass door or window.

GRUNDFOS DORMITORY
in Aarhus, Denmark

Designed by CEBRA
Photo© Mikkel Frost

The local based architecture firm CEBRA has developed a 12-story dormitory building for 200 students in the Engineering College of Aarhus, Denmark. The Grundfos dormitory, which sits on the harbor front development, with 7,000 inhabitants within an 80,000-square-meter tract of land, is a pilot project to transform this former industrial harbor into a dynamic community.

The dormitory building looks like book shelves with different heights filled with colorful-covered books by the daytime. These "book shelves" encircle an atrium, where the architects have furnished mirrors on the surrounding corridors to create an aesthetically-pleasing space. These walls reflect the setting and activities in the building while enlarging the visual effect of the narrow indoor space, which also are added a sense of liveliness by applying color stripes of yellow, orange and red from the dormitory doors. They are also there to introduce sunlight down into the concealed atrium from a large skylight by reflection, thus reducing the energy consumption of the building.

BIGSHELF + MINIHATTAN

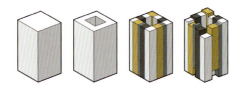

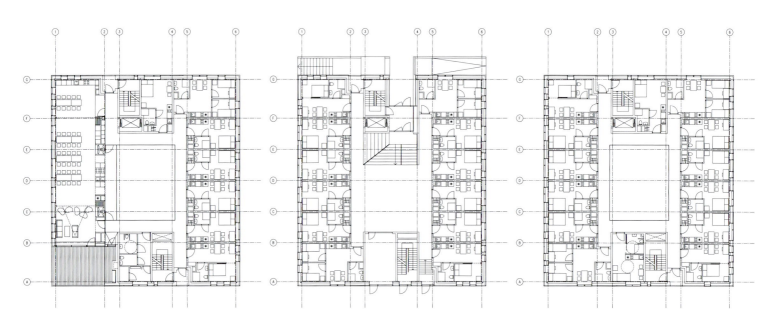

ACADEMIE MWD
in Dilbeek, Belgium

Designed by Carlos Arroyo Arquitectos
Photo© Miguel de Guzmán

The west part of Brussels has an informal cultural capital in Dilbeek, home of the Westrand Cultural Centre and its various facilities. The Academie MWD is situated at a uniquely varied crossroads in the center of Dilbeek and offers education in music, theater and dance, as well as an auditorium-theater.

The building for Academie MWD is surrounded by a main square with the city hall and local restaurants in the south, Wolfsputten, a protected forest in the north, in the west Westrand Cultural Center and a Brutalist community center by the architect Alfons Hoppenbrouwers who was skilled in using colors, and the east a series of quaint suburban villas. The Madrid-based architect Carlos Arroyo had a distinct challenge to erect a building with a quality of its own, which can make sense from all directions.

To harmonize the different surrounding situations, Arroyo modulated the scale and form of the building. The jagged edge of the roof mimics those of the homes across the street, rising gradually to the cantilevered auditorium at one end, and rising up to look face to face with the monumental volumes of Westrand Cultural Center.

Arroyo also used image and texture to dematerialize a volume that would otherwise impose on the neighbouring villas. The compact form reduces the surface/volume ratio and energy loss. The façade seems to blend into the forest, and the series of vertical fins on the façade running from top to bottom are in fact a gigantic piece of Op-Art, reflecting the images of the surroundings. The interior of the building is painted white except the linoleum floor, maximizing the reflection of the natural daylight. By night, the LED lights illuminate the fins sparsely, creating a delicate tapestry as a backdrop to the street in the dark night.

TONY'S FARM
in Shanghai, China

● ●

Designed by playze
Photo© Bartasz Kolonko

Tony's Farm is the biggest organic food farm in Shanghai, which produces OFDC certified vegetables and fruits. Its vision is to integrate consumers and promote a natural lifestyle.

To link the activities of the staff with visitors of the farm, the Shanghai-based playze developed a container building complex, which combines a main reception, a lobby (reserved for future hotel rooms) and a VIP area, with new offices and an existing warehouse, where the fruits and vegetables are packed. The building provides transparency within the manufacturing process. It supports the vision of involving the visitor and helps to reinforce consumer confidence in products of the farm. The building design, which is driven by the concept of sustainability, combined with its iconic qualities, promotes the main principle of Tony's Farm.

The cubing of the containers follows spatial and climatic demands. To adapt to local climate, the building is designed to meet standards of permeability and insulation. The building is a three-story high vertical volume, which can open on three sides to dissolve the framed box. Details were developed to maintain the stringent appearance of the raw-tectonic structure. In order to provide easy accessibility, playze was challenged to distribute the containers irregularly and finally coped with this issue by developing a modular system.

In an effort to reduce energy loss and protect the environment, several strategies have been developed to reduce energy consumption of the building. The original container doors have been perforated to serve as external fans, and a geothermal heat pump delivers energy for air conditioning and floor heating systems. Controlled ventilation helps optimize air exchange rates, thus to minimize energy loss through uncontrolled aeration, while the use of LED lighting reduces electricity consumption. Savings on building materials also help minimize the so-called "grey energy".

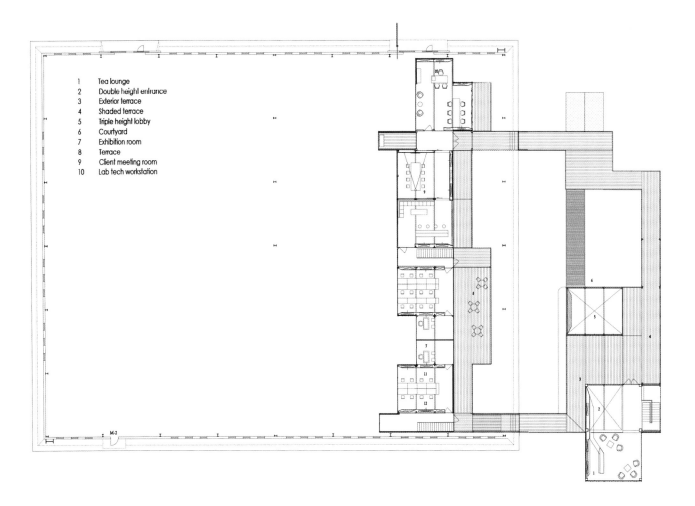

1   Tea lounge
2   Double height entrance
3   Exterior terrace
4   Shaded terrace
5   Triple height lobby
6   Courtyard
7   Exhibition room
8   Terrace
9   Client meeting room
10 Lab tech workstation

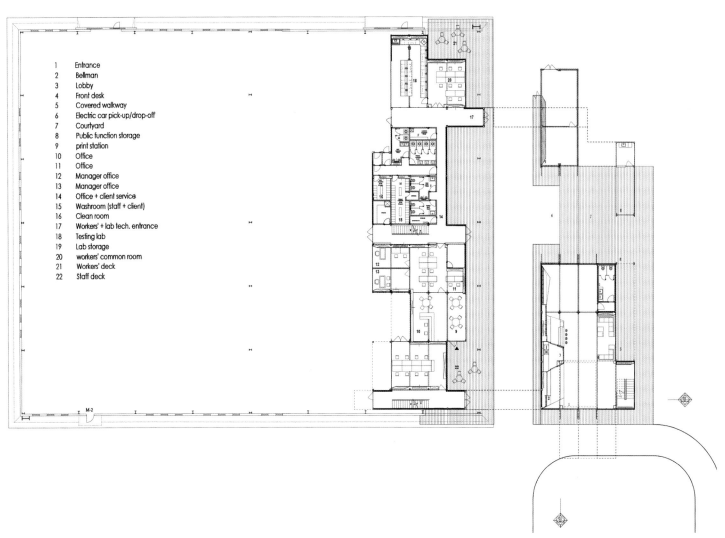

1   Entrance
2   Bellman
3   Lobby
4   Front desk
5   Covered walkway
6   Electric car pick-up/drop-off
7   Courtyard
8   Public function storage
9   print station
10   Office
11   Office
12   Manager office
13   Manager office
14   Office + client service
15   Washroom (staff + client)
16   Clean room
17   Workers' + lab tech. entrance
18   Testing lab
19   Lab storage
20   workers' common room
21   Workers' deck
22   Staff deck

NMA ADMINISTRATION—ARM ARCHITETURE
in Canberra, Australia

Designed by ARM Architecture
Photo© John Gollings

The initial concept for the National Museum of Australia was to organise a collection of structures expressed as puzzle pieces, each with a differentiated, stylised appearance. This strategy meant the scheme has remained conceptually incomplete, a work in progress toward the articulation of the Australian experience.

The new adminstration wing adds to the accretion of puzzle pieces—it is expressed, quite literally, as a colourful puzzle piece, slotting in between the old wing and the annexe. Using heat-mapping patterns (as often employed in archival and curatorial works) the external coloured, ceramic-tiled skin of the extension blends the hue of the green cladding of the administration wing with that of the pale yellow of annexe bricks, providing continuity between the two.

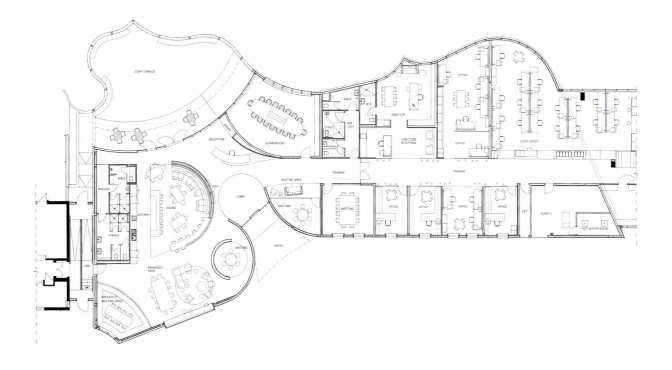

The overlaid coding and organisational technique of QR codes (Quick Response) provides a layer of information and details, where actual messages and data can be gathered by museum visitors.

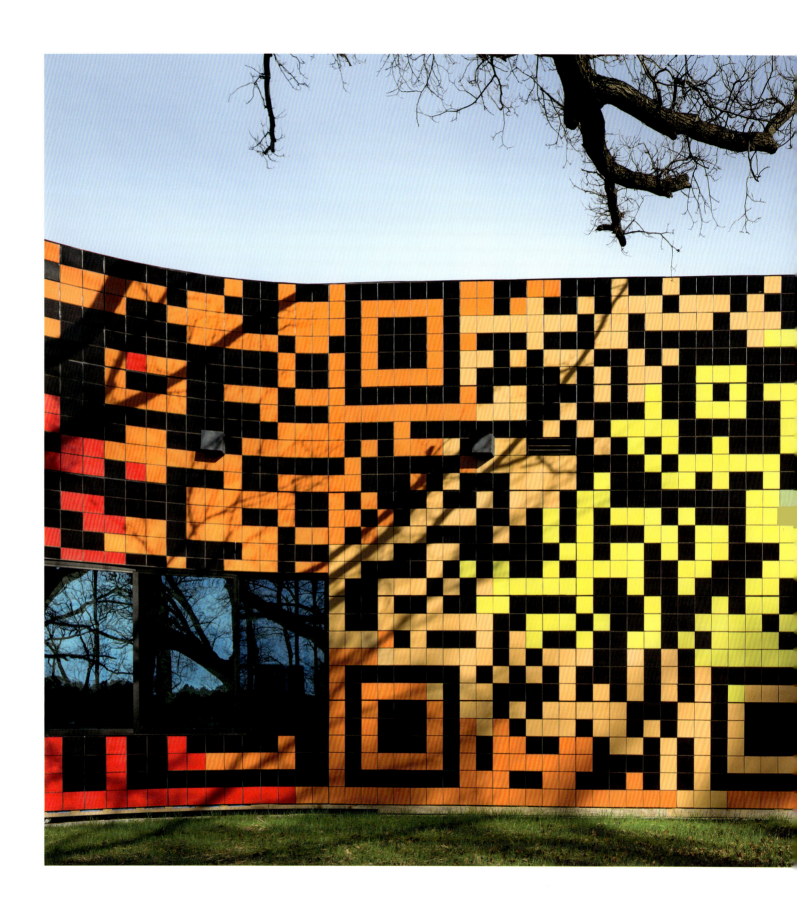

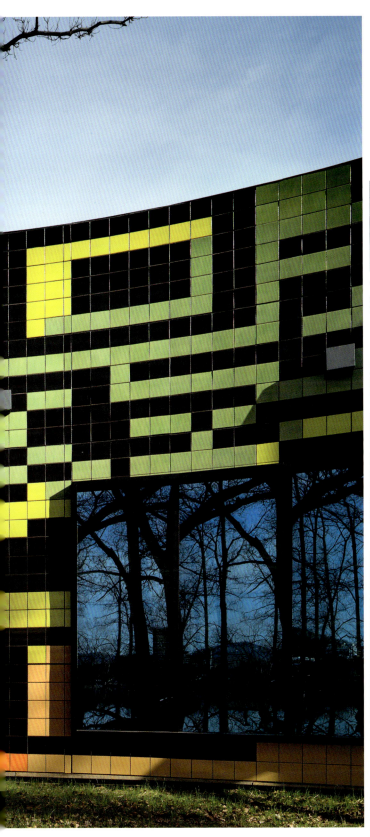

KUGGEN
in Örnsköldsvik, Sweden

Designed by Wingårdh Arkitektkontor AB thru Gert Wingårdh and Jonas Edblad
Photo© Åke E:son Lindman and Tord-Rikard Söderström

This cylindrical, distinctive building in the middle of a town square is for the commercial estate agent, Chalmersfastigheter AB, an urban planning space intended for informal meetings, with roots in Italian Renaissance. The form offers lots of floor spaces in relation to the amount of exposed exterior wall surfaces, and the upper floors project out over the lower—more on the south side than on the north, so that the building partially shades itself when the sun is high in the sky. A rotating screen shades the top floors, following the sun's path around the building. The triangular shaped windows let in the light where it's needed most—from the ceiling, from where it can reach deep into the core of the building.

Its iconic brocade of glazed terracotta panels take on different appearances depending on the viewing angle and the changing daylight conditions. The red colors refer to the industrial paint that is closely associated with the wharfs and the harbor. Here and there they meet a contrasting green patch, as in an autumn leaf. These details change the building's character from one side to another, and over the course of the day. The consistency of the façade has been achieved by stainless steel clips and the unit length of the panels varies from 570mm to 2,800mm in eight different colors.

TISSE MÉTIS ÉGAL
in Montréal, Canada

Designed by PLUX.5

Photo© Alexandre Guilbeault

As part of the Métis-sur-Montréal event, in its 4th consecutive year, Château Ramezay and the Reford Gardens presented the exhibit Tisse Métis Égal created by the collective PLUX.5. This imposing architectural structure, perched on the grassy pedestal at Place De La Dauversière, offers a surprising new perspective on the city's urban landscape.

Erected in the heart of the historical district, this contemporary installation acts as a bright colored filter that transforms perception of the surrounding environment.

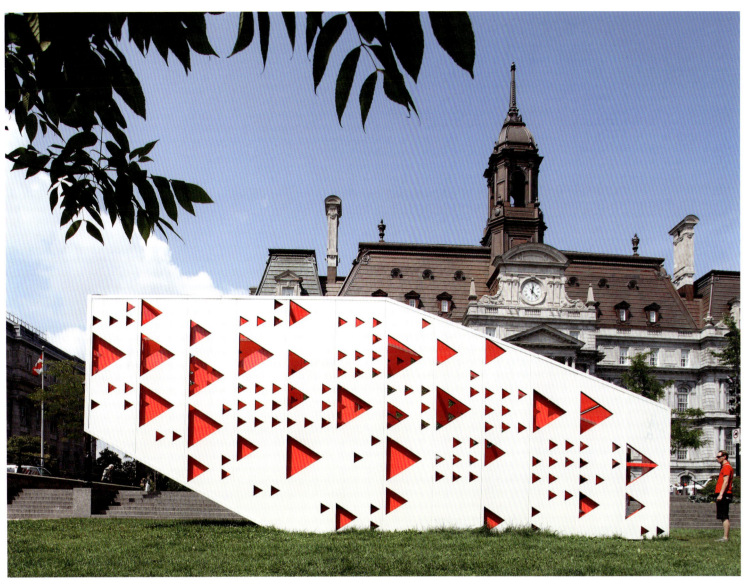

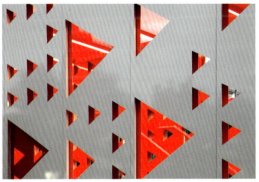

Its walls, perforated with a scatter of triangular patterns—cleverly evocative of traditional weaving, particularly the ornamentation of the arrowhead sash—draw a striking parallel with Québec's past. Inside, visitors are immersed in a play of shadows and light that shapes their understanding of the work and its surrounding elements. Tisse Métis Égal is a tribute to Québec's history, offering an interpretation of its traditions through a contemporary lens.

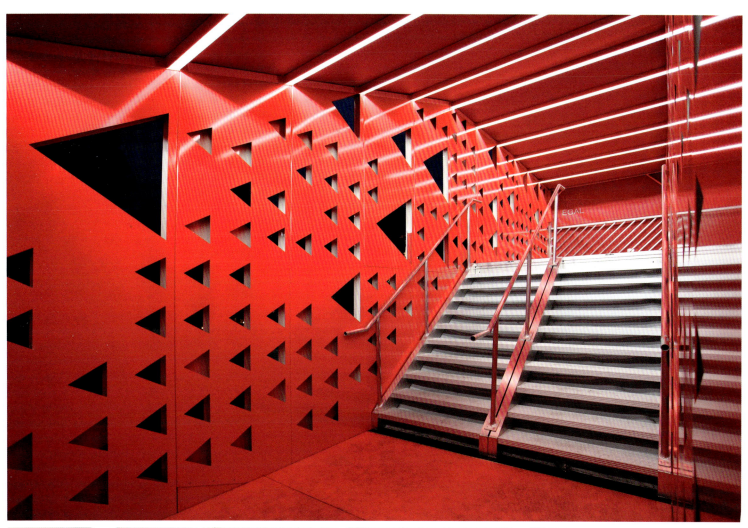

LOLLIPOP HOUSE
in Gyeonggi-Do, Korea

Designed by Moonbalsso of Moon Hoon
Photo© Nam goong Sun

Evoking the imagery of a lollipop with alternating pink and white rings, this single family residence for Giheung-Gu, in Korea conceals seven storeys of internal living spaces. Designed by Seoul-based practice Moon Hoon, this segmented elevation is organized around a central stair that branches to seven living levels. Wrapped in a colorful façade of metal panels, the coloring choice is a strong statement for the unusual residence along with conjuring up images of a child's favorite treat. Accessed from the central stair, each space is naturally illuminated with a series of skylights, including the lowest level, a half-basement which contains the study. The client urged Moon Hoon to explore the idea of multiple living planes, which has resulted in a skip floor setup with a study, a living area, a kitchen and a dining area, a master bedroom, the children's bedroom, a attic playroom and a upper level room, stemming from the circulation core. An atrium runs the height of the house and allows natural light to illuminate the interiors.

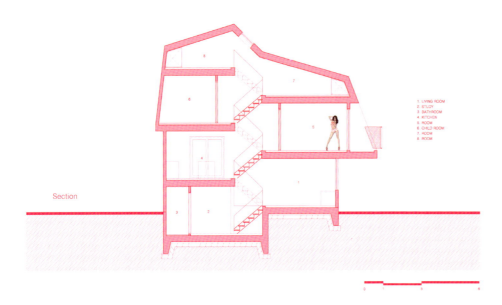

Section

1. LIVING ROOM
2. STUDY
3. BATHROOM
4. KITCHEN
5. ROOM
6. CHILD ROOM
7. ROOM
8. ROOM

The design started with explorations of rising stairs and spirals. Due to budget limitation, the ideas were simplified into a practical skip floor format which wraps around an interior void to form an atrium.

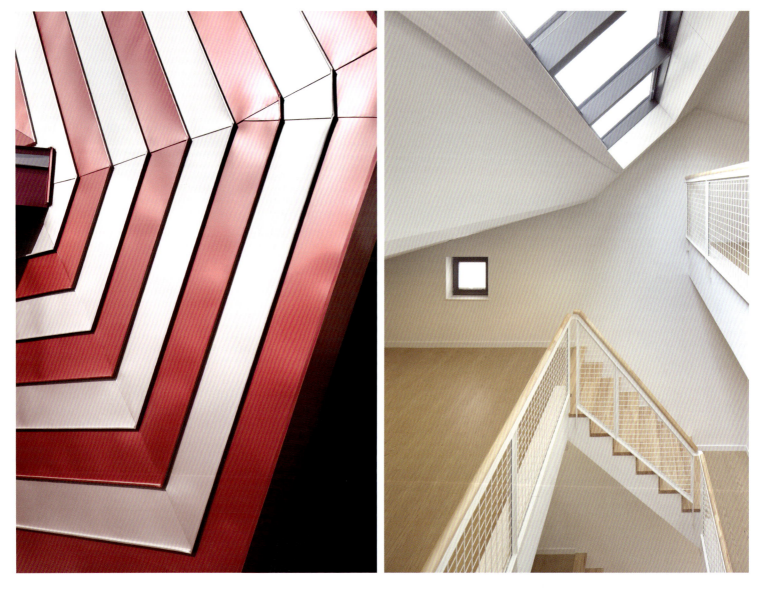

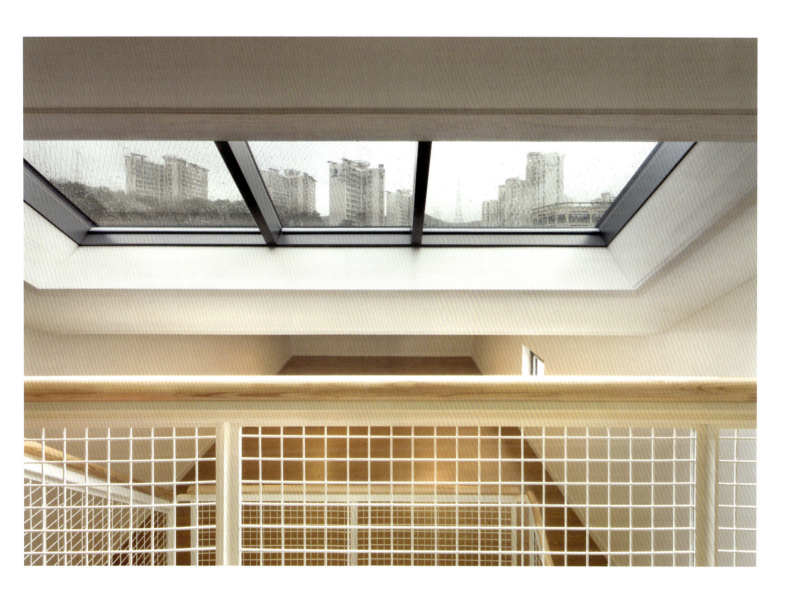

SUGAMO SHINKIN BANK EKODA BRANCH
in Tokyo, Japan

Designed by emmanuelle moureaux architecture + design
Photo© Daisuke Shima/ Nacasa & Partners Inc.

The Ekoda branch is another brightly colored annex created by Tokyo-based French architect Emmanuelle Moureaux for Sugamo Shinkin Bank. Moureaux's concept of "shikiri", literally "to divide space with color" has been employed again in this project for the Japanese financial chain, which aims to "create a bank the customers feel happy to visit".

Centered on the concept of "a rainbow shower" Moureaux has not only brought joyfulness within the bank, but also extended it to its surroundings.

To emphasize the bank's proximity to the activities in the commercial district of Ekoda, Tokyo, the architect merged the exterior and interior of the building by using several strategies. The boldly designed façade of the building is surrounded by a lounge-like area filled with 29 colorful nine meter tall sticks puncturing the air. Reflected on the glazed façade, these exterior sticks blend with the 19 interior ones. The exterior is pushed further inside the bank as a courtyard leads to the bank's services. When the bank is open, the glass panels pivot open to let visitors through to an indoor terrace filled with colorful furniture to lend a cheerful atmosphere to the bank.

As the design team explained, "This rainbow shower brings color and some room for playfulness back to the town." The Ekoda branch creates a brilliant and joyful landscape that connects to the surroundings.

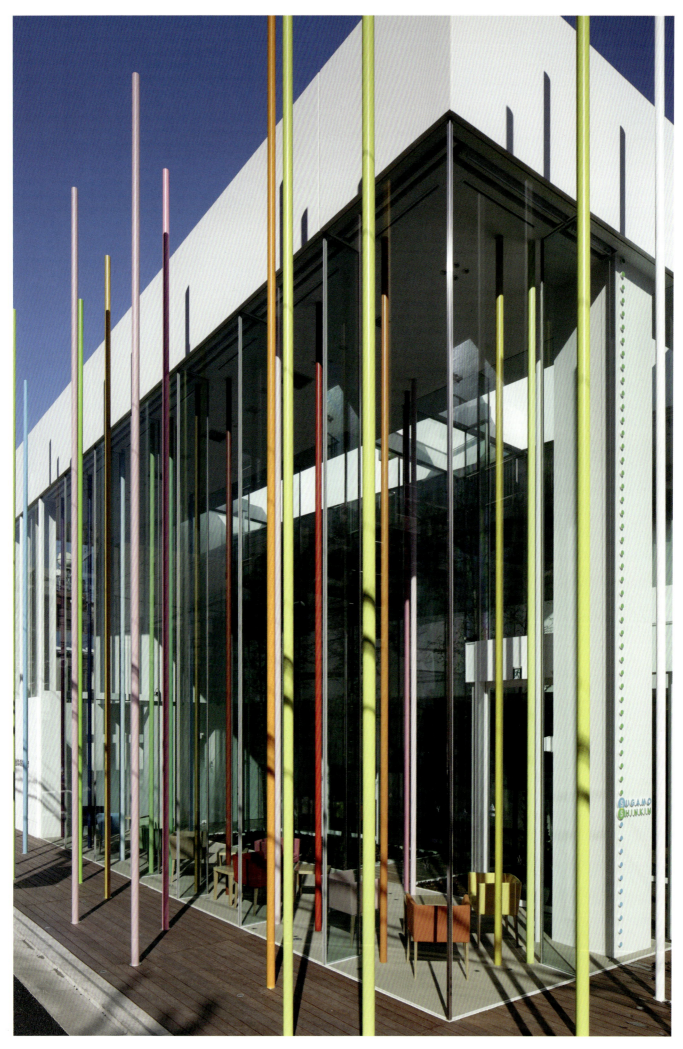

THE GOURMET TEA SHOP
in São Paulo, Brazil

Designed by Alan Chu
Photo© Djan Chu

Pop-up shops seem to be all the rage nowadays and many different types of businesses such as online stores and brands not well-known yet come into the game with creative storefronts. This pop-up shop designed by Brazilian architect Alan Chu is the third branch for local tea brand The Gourmet Tea. Inspired by the brightly colored packing for the tea brand, Alan Chu used movable flat panels on a multi-colored wall to create this secret tea shop in a São Paulo shopping center.

With only a 25-square-meter space, the tea shop exterior is coated with Formica in bright colors concealed behind a hinged flap. The counter is designed to be able to slide forward from a purple hatch, while shelves for products can roll out from behind a grey panel and a cupboard emerges from behind a large brown door.

FRONTAL VIEW
OPEN STORE

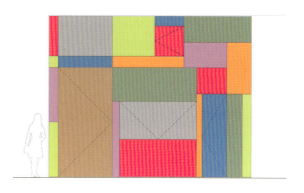

FRONTAL VIEW
CLOSED STORE

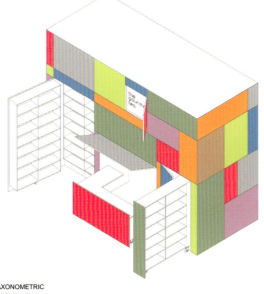

AXONOMETRIC
OPEN SHOP

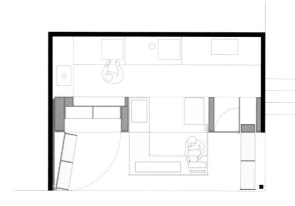

PLAN

É PRÁ PONCHA
in Oporto, Portugal

Designed by António Fernandez Architects
Photo© José Campos

Portuguese design firm António Fernandez Architects has conceived the É Prá Poncha bar that resembles a multi-colored cavern, taking inspiration from natural caves. The club and bar is located on Porto's famous Rua da Galeria de Paris, providing all the rich vibrant tones of the city. The ceiling of the nightclub is covered with horizontal strata made of lacquered MDF, mimicking water drippings from melting ice or eroding limestone hanging from a cave's ceiling.

"Simultaneously these strata waves organically shape various spaces and create voids and chambers," says architect António Fernandez. "They develop support services to the bar, like the clean pantry, the dirty pantry, toilets and storage rooms."

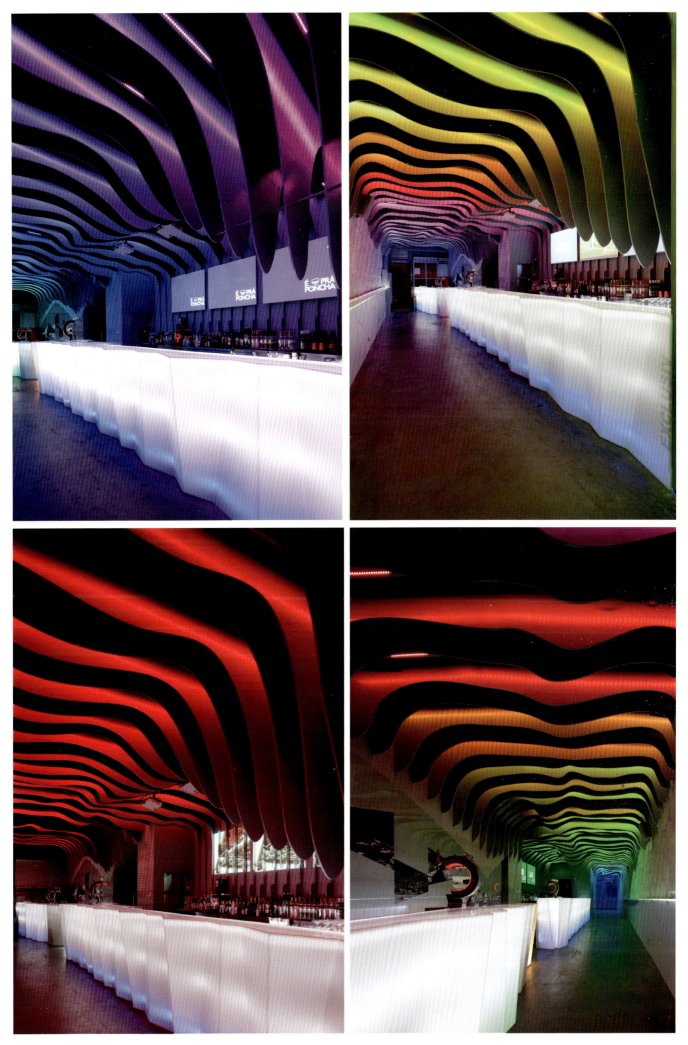

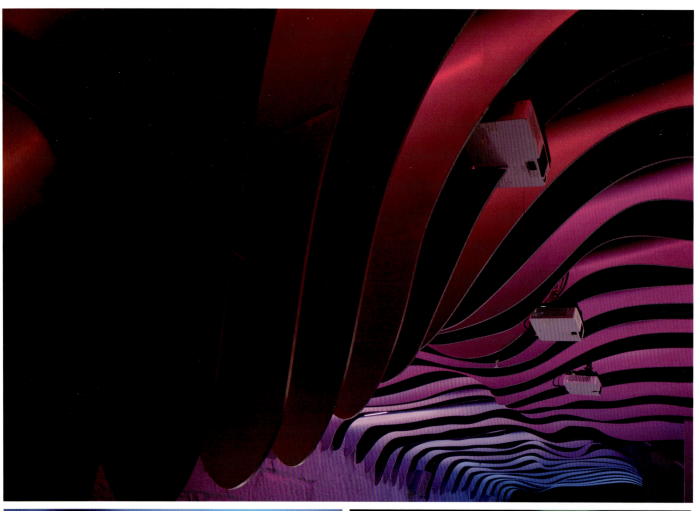

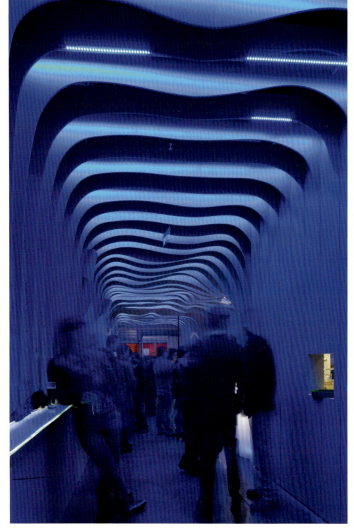

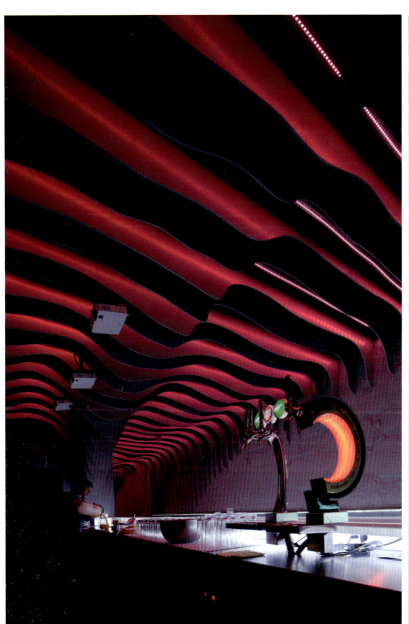
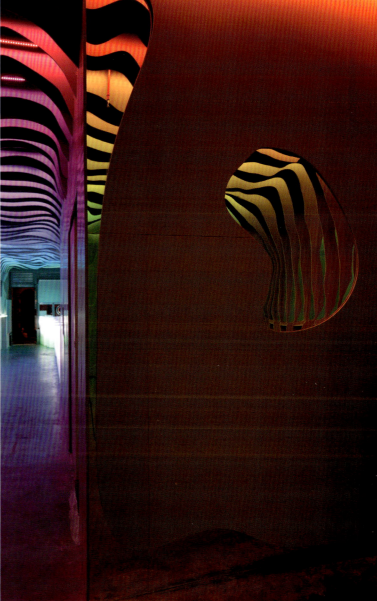

The bar design is alluring with its constantly changing LED light system, which make the space shift from bright red to icy blue. With the hues of fire and ice, the bar brings a wonderful stream in within the narrow space, provoking clients' emotions.

IL FIORE DI NOVEMBRE
in Milan, Italy

Designed by Fabio Novembre
Photo© Pasquale Formisano

Italian designer Fabio Novembre has created mosaic-covered sections representing a flower at the Triennale Design Museum in Milan, Italy. These flower sections separate the space into different areas so as to create rooms for each work in display.

"Everything can be done starting from a flower," Novembre explained, "A flower is a symbolic abstraction, a beauty which may be expressed through shapes and colors." Novembre's flower adopts a dreamy approach, creating a romantic atmosphere for the exhibition.

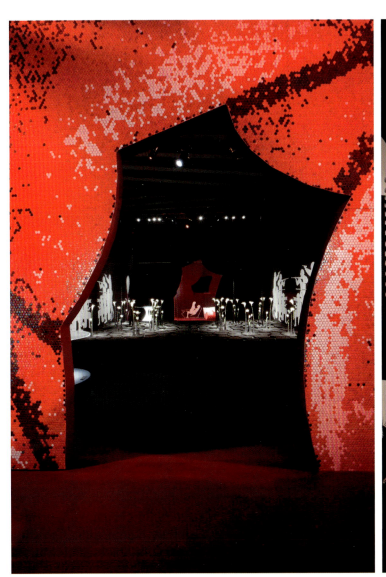

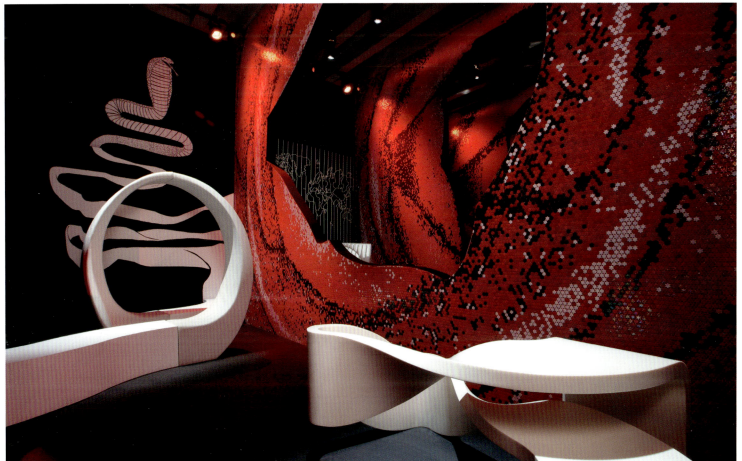

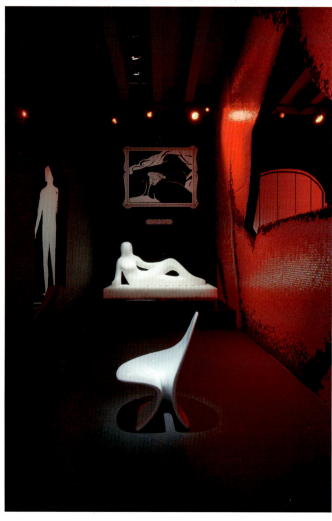

PKO BANK POLSKI WARSAW BRANCH
in Warsaw, Poland

Designed by Robert Majkut Design
Photo© Szymon Polański

This project designed by Warsaw-headquartered Robert Majkut Design was the first branch for Poland's biggest financial institution PKO Bank Polski which engages in creating a chain of branches dedicated to the prestigious services of private banking. The branch is divided into two functional areas including customer service zones and the back-office.

The starting point was the Bank's modernized logo in its elegant color version—black, white and gold, which created a set for the interior design. The inspiring decorative motif, a grid of sinusoidal lines was turned into a tri-dimensional pattern by using parametric design software.

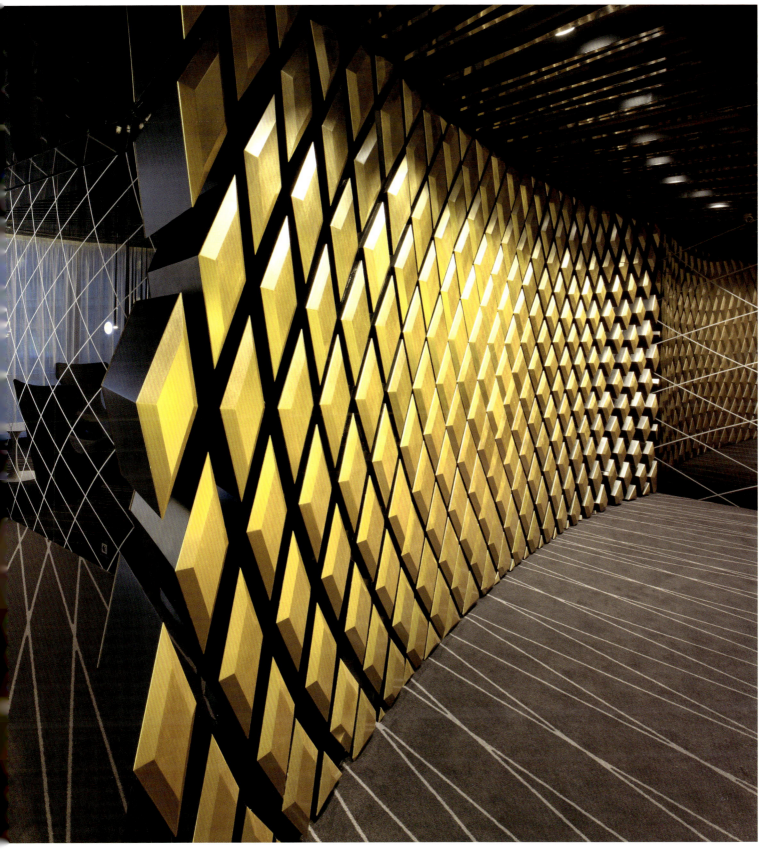

The furnishings and finishing materials were custom designed for this particular facility. The bold usage of a minimalistic palette of colors, where gold balances the strong contrast between black and white with its unique decorative qualities, brings a warm and noble space referring to a bank branch with values such as prestige, stability and prosperity.

ALIOR BANK PRIVATE BANKING
in Poland

Designed by Robert Majkut Design
Photo© OLO Studio

Polish designer Robert Majkut has developed a characteristic identity for Alior Bank private banking branches in Poland, based on the stylized face of an angel from an old drawing. The designer wanted to distinguish private banking facilities from retail service upon the bank's market launch.

The corporate color palette is built on black, copper and graphite gray. The main geometric motif can be found in the graphical lines shown in the rescaled logo in the reception zone, and also present in the engraving of the angel figure. It is seen as a tribute to the Dutch painter Piet Mondrian and also a reference to the Bauhaus school.

The arrangement has brought together the office interiors and a unique retro style into the modern banking center, and built it into an elegant and inviting whole to meet customer expectations.

MY SQUASH CLUB

in Poznań, Poland

• •

Designed by Kreacja Przestrzeni
Photo© Paweł Penkala

This sports center designed by Polish design studio Kreacja Przestrzeni houses a unique and clean interior that is comfortable and practical. My Squash Club is not designed for gym alone—there are also beautifully designed rooms to relax, like a bar, and aerobic/art classrooms.

The project detaches from the convention of sport centers. The club coated with radiant sky blue color provides functional areas with comfortable furnishings and well-appointed equipment. The fantastic lamps made by Puff-Buf Studio and Daria Burlińska create a characteristic lighting for the interior. The white resin floors and the consistency of colors in the clear space are supplemented with blue furnishings, making My Squash a modern, fresh and surprising experience.

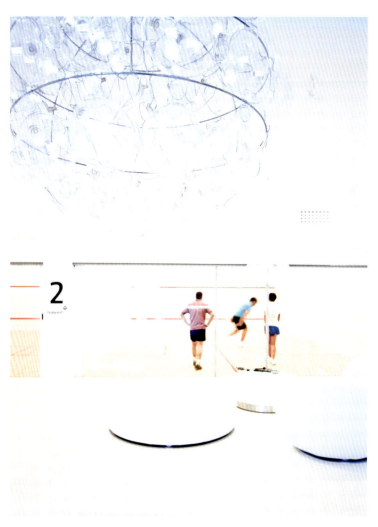

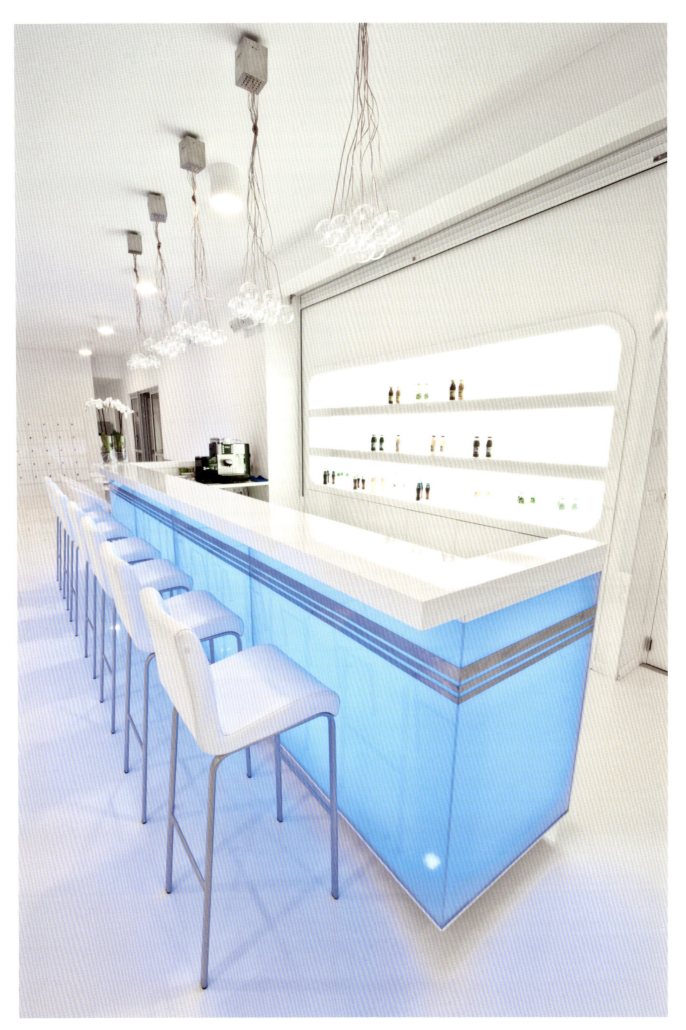

IBM SOFTWARE EXECUTIVE BRIEFING CENTER
in Rome, Italy

Designed by Iosa Ghini Associati
Photo© Santi Caleca

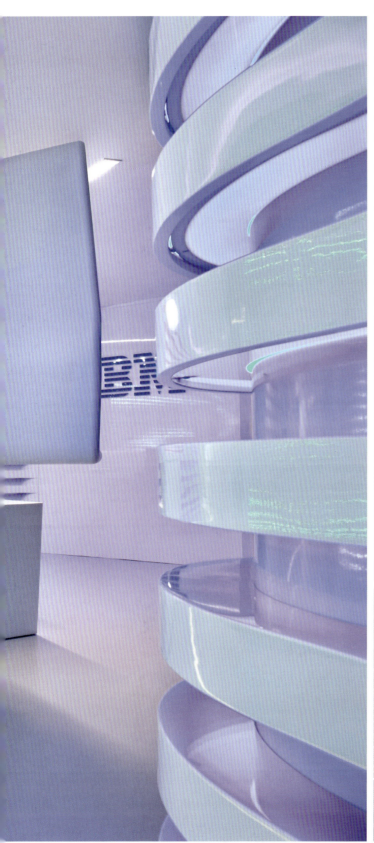

IBM Software Executive Briefing Center in Rome has been entirely renovated and has significantly expanded its area. The project designed by Iosa Ghini Associati, elaborates IBM's iconic eight-striped logo in an innovative and fascinating way.

The most challenging part in designing this project was to create a contemporary interior with its original values intact along with the current vision and goals for a long-established brand. The Bologna's architect Massimo Iosa Ghini has renovated the technology company with architectural elements to support the spatial design requested by IBM.

The parallel lines serve as the backdrop to the space and provide rhythm within the interior. The interior is lit up with the strategically placed colored lighting, which forms a grid pattern and reflects against the smooth ceiling, walls and floor. The ceiling with recessed cove lighting forms an interesting shape against the surrounding linear design. Few of the light fixtures can be seen and most of the space is lit indirectly, which establishes a connection to the innovative values of IBM's products and services.

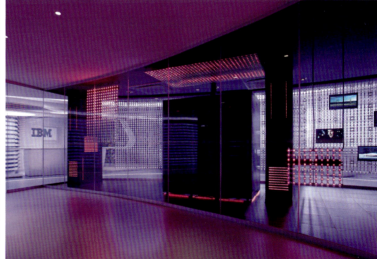

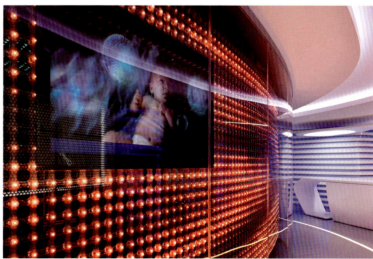

The clean and smooth innovative IBM office speaks clearly about the brand, making itself the signage to communicate with the visitors.

YMS HAIR SALON
in Ljubljana, Slovenia

Designed by Kitsch Nitsch
Photo© Miha Brodaric/Multipraktik

Slovenian design duo Kitsch Nitsch furnished the new YMS salon in Slovenian with a post modernistic design, triggering a flashback to the glorious 70s and 80s.

The project was commissioned by Mič Styling, whose new YMS Salon line targets a younger audience. In wanting to "keep things as wild as possible," Kitsch-Nitsch filled the space with 70s and 80s style furnishings and textures to shape a retro yet youthful image for the hair salon. The interior is adorned with clashing hues, vivid graphics and retro prints that were inspired by haircuts.

The salon areas are arranged with shelving for products and magazines, decorated with vivid signage. The irregular mirrors on the walls framed in colorful ribbons are functional yet decorative, adding a youthful feeling. Several sculptures in bright white are like performers on the small stage of the salon, bringing it a dramatic effect.

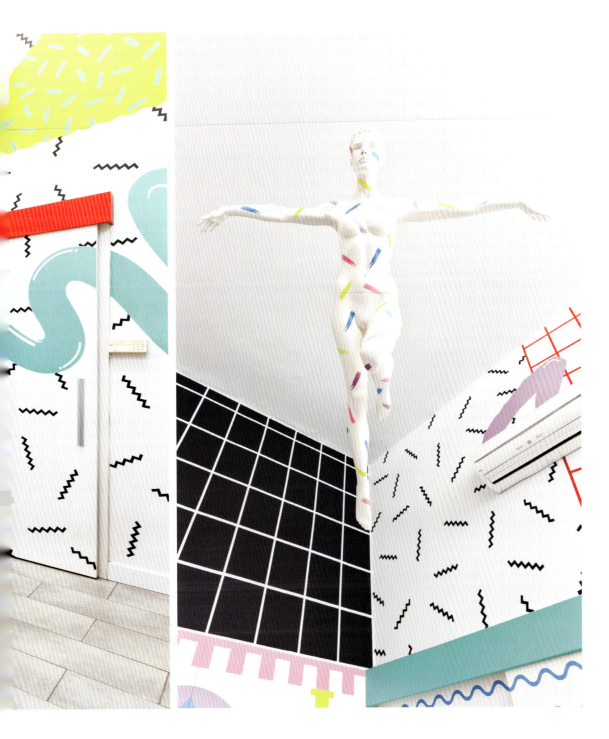

CONGA ROOM NOKIA CENTER
in California, USA

Designed by Belzberg Architects
Photo© Benny Chan

The Conga Room, in its new location at LA Live in downtown Los Angeles across from the Staples Center, is the city's premier Latin nightclub. The space features today's hottest Latin performers in its 14,000-square-foot space, which includes a restaurant, three distinct bars, patio seating, and a VIP lounge and private room. In addition, the club hosts LA TV and world-renowned DJs adjacent to the stage and above the crowd, adding even more excitement to the ambiance. The club design's intent is to be true to the energy and vibrant color of the Latin community, to pay homage to its roots and deep history while infusing it with Los Angeles' fervent modern lifestyle.

For over a decade, the Conga room has been a Los Angeles cultural landmark. The Latin live music and dance venue was LA's center for Salsa and Rumba. The original location closed in 2006 with the goal of opening a new venue in the new "LA Live" complex in Downtown Los Angeles.

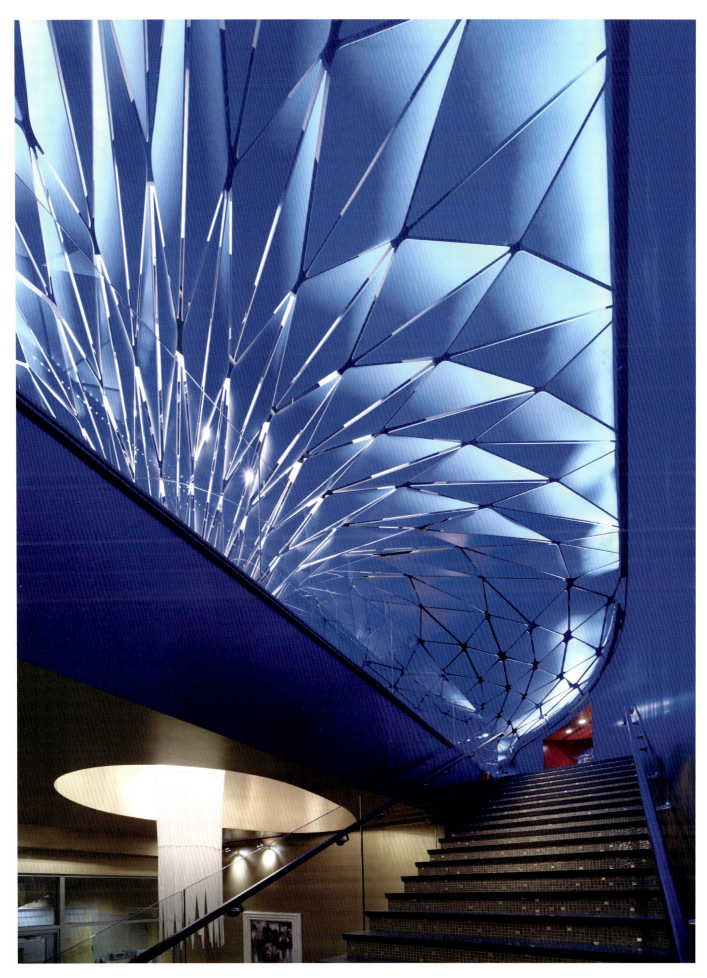

As if coordinating and blending the varied programs and styles together wasn't challenging enough, the space, originally planned for office use, had a very low and equipment-filled ceiling to negotiate and needed to operate within a mixed-use building. As a consequence, three major factors drive the design process: First, the space had to be acoustically isolated from the rest of the building while simultaneously performing acoustically for its performers and patrons. Second, it was anticipated that the club would continuously be filled to its full capacity, thus most conventional architectural devices—walls and floors, would be obscured by patrons. Finally, the club was located on the second floor of the building off the main plaza, a classic foible for restaurant and club operators who commonly find difficulties in beguiling patrons up a flight of stairs or elevators. The solution was to use the ceiling to perform as the spatial organizer, the primary acoustical isolator/amplifier and event attractor.

In an effort to meet the client's desire for an aesthetic that would reflect the vibrancy and dynamism of Latin culture, the ceiling surface, fashioned from a series of Computer Numerically Controlled (CNC)-milled, painted plywood panels, was created by assembling

diamond patterns, which were initially derived from the classic Cuban Rumba dance step. Each panel represents a "petal" while the grouping of six "petals" makes "a flower". Parametric 3D modeling and building performance software aided in the proliferation of the "flowers" on a unified, undulating surface that wanes and blossoms, distinguishing each of the unique environments within the club. As the event attractor, the ceiling panels converges into a 20-foot-tall glowing "tornado" that penetrates the dance floor, inviting and guiding patrons up to the activities in the club. To further intensify the experience, the room boastes an integral, state-of-the-art LED lighting system which gives the ceiling the ability to change colors and atmosphere at the push of a button or even react to, in real time, the rhythms and sounds of the music, becoming an active participant in the scene.

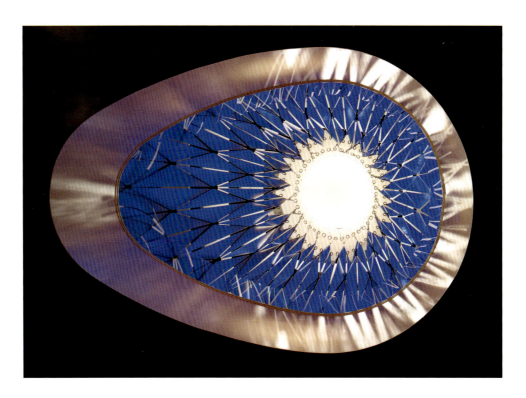

In addition to aesthetic concerns, the ceiling had to mitigate complex building infrastructure, goals specific to that of a live music venue. Multiple lighting systems, audio visual systems, mechanical systems and fire/life safety systems, among many others, had to be considered. As previously mentioned, various acoustical considerations had to be explored and controlled. The parametric design model allowed the porosity of the ceiling to be manipulated based on feedback from performance, based on data collected from various acoustic analysis software packages. In effect, the ceiling was not an infinitely thin surface extended to all corners but rather a deep surface, layering and mitigating multiple constituencies to create a complex piece of building infrastructure, providing both a dynamic visual environment as well as a great place to listen to music.

SNOG SOHO
in London, UK

Designed by Cinimod Studio
Photo© Cinimod Studio

Cinimod Studio has created a compact but high impact presence for the second store of Snog Pure Frozen Yogurt located at the busy Marylebone High Street. Generous window seats provide a perfect place to relax whilst momentarily pausing between the contrasting environments of the busy street outdoors and the surreal colorful and animated indoor Snog environment. There are always new elements of design and materials in each and every Snog store where the brand continues to refine its boutique retail experience.

The main feature of this Marylebone Snog store is the globe ceiling, which came from the desire to expand on the "digital sky" concept that Cinimod Studio had created at the first Snog store in South Kensington. Cinimod Studio developed this design idea aiming at evoking the feeling of a perfect, never-ending summer. The interior is deliberately quirky, with a photographic grass floor and a bubbling sky which continuously adjust the mood of the store. The bright pink brand color is featured outdoors on the fascia signage panel which features an array of vertical slats in pink acrylic.

SNOG KINGS ROAD

in London, UK

Designed by Cinimod Studio
Photo© Cinimod Studio

Cinimod studio has delivered their sixth Snog Pure Frozen Yogurt store, and as always, design and technology boundaries have been pushed to deliver a unique retail space.

The Chelsea store presented unique design challenges that included a deep shop unit with a relatively narrow shop front. This led to the Cinimod design team seeking innovative ways to create a highly visible store that would deliver an eye-catching high street presence using a fusion between sculptured architecture and lighting elements. Building on design explorations from previous Snog stores, Cinimod has taken integrated furniture and lighting design to new levels.

Highly visible from outside is the "Ribbon Ceiling" of undulating light. The complex form was derived using parametric software to create the smooth rippling form that varies in depth and pitch spanning the entire store plan. Cinimod Studio has a proven passion for experimenting with lighting control systems, with a desire to keep pushing the interactive and generative nature of our digital lighting media content. For the Snog Chelsea store, Cinimod deployed a new lighting control system by amBX. This responds in real-time to the store's music system, creating dynamic color movements across the ribbon ceiling that are perfectly in tune with the music. This ensures that the ceiling colors never appear static or repetitive, and instead are in a state of continuous responsiveness to the acoustic environment.

The studio's expertise in LED lighting was further tested by the introduction of a 100% LED lighting solution for the whole store. This provides unparalleled energy efficiency and full

controllability over the exact quality and brightness of light. Cinimod Studio turned to Philips for their assistance in delivering this ambitious scheme. The resulting quality of light is remarkably fresh, healthy and natural feeling, with the brightness linked to the main control system to allow automatic subtle variations throughout the day.

The seating within the store is focused on a single over-size organic bench, fabricated as a single piece to achieve the smooth and seamless continuous curvature that provides its distinct form.

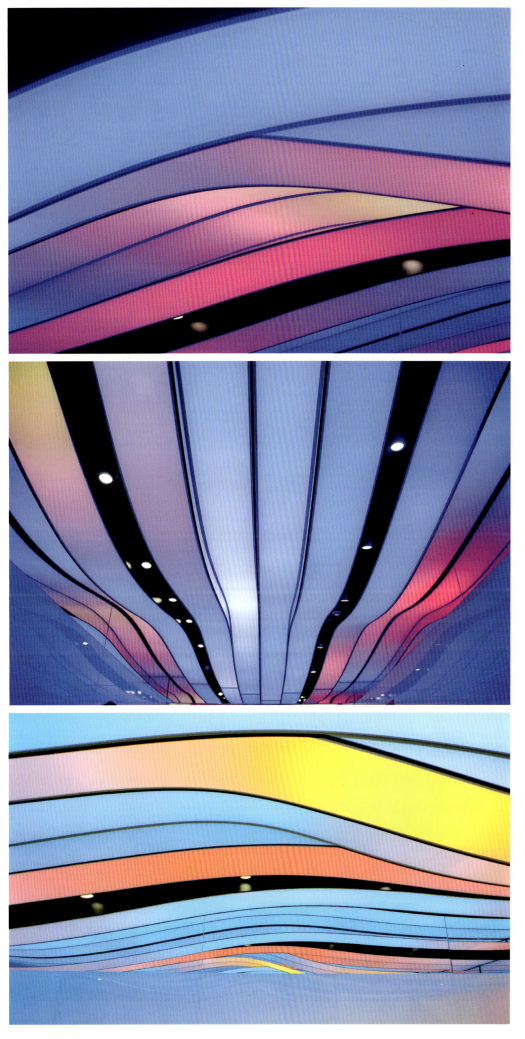

BLACK BOX
in Timisoara, Romania

Designed by Parasite Studio
Photo© Dumitrascu Marius, Parasite Studio

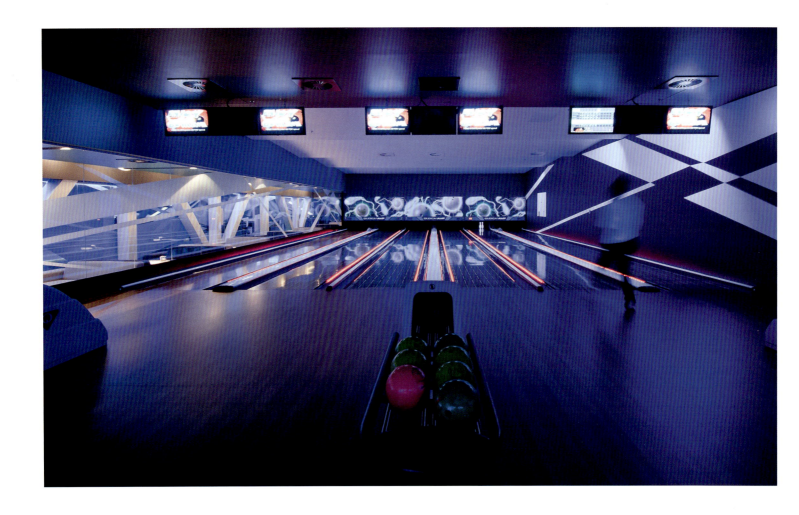

The Romanian nightclub Black Box designed by Parasite Studio, as its name suggests, shows geometric spatial elements based on the concept of a black box.

Starting from the unique concept, Parasite Studio wanted to design a concealed world inside the black box within the existing unconventional layout. The interior is wrapped in illuminated color strips which run along the walls and the floor, twisting the perception of the existing steel structure.

The lighting system within the space is dynamic and vivid. With a dark blue backdrop, the illuminant colors give off a radiant glow.

The club is divided into several zones such as a bar, technical areas, a bowling area and a smoking area, with a large central cylinder-like skylight allowing natural light to filter into the interior, adding to LED lighting. The furniture is custom designed for this project to assist the black box theme, while the carpet with strips on the floor acts like a map to offer directions in the illusive space.

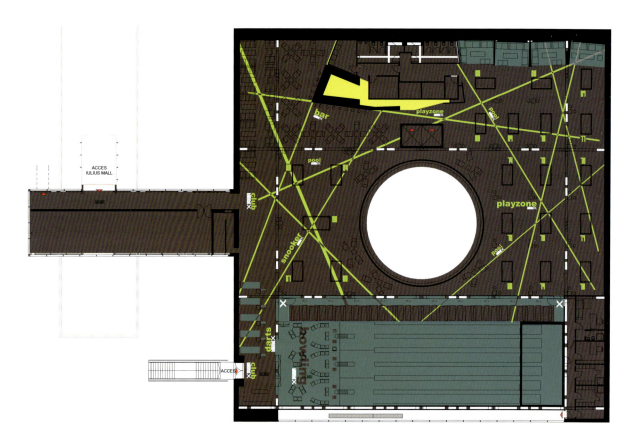

ACCES
IULIUS MALL

ACCES

0   10

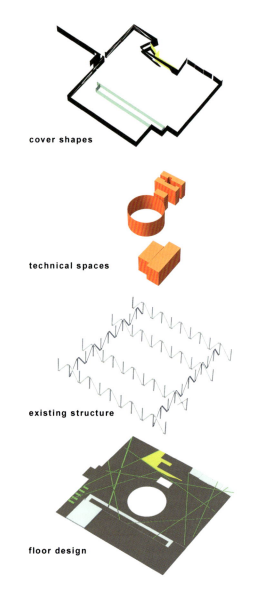

cover shapes

technical spaces

existing structure

floor design

ING BANK OFFICES
in Romania

Designed by Corvin Cristian
Photo© Corvin Cristian

The designer drew inspiration from the Dutch artistic movement De Stijl, Dutch for "The Style", which has also been known as "neo-plasticism" to design the ING Bank offices.

Romanian designer Corvin Cristian has completed the ING Bank offices in Romania, in collaboration with designer Matei Niculescu. The interiors are enveloped with white flooring, upon which is painted a grid of vertical and horizontal black lines and filled with three primary colors, mimicking famous De Stijl contributor, Mondrian. The corridors also feature replicas of Mondrian's paintings in the original size, by the same technique.

The display and lighting recalls an art gallery, adding to the theatrical yet cosy atmosphere.

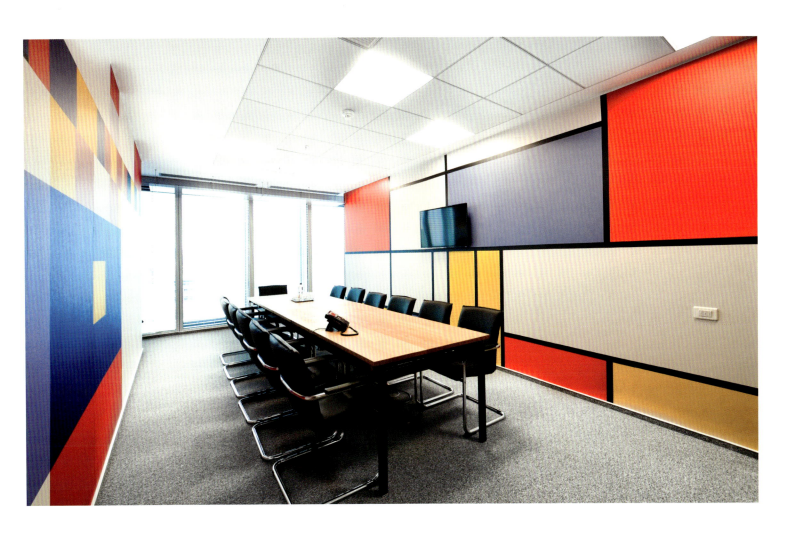

BANGKOK UNIVERSITY STUDENT LOUNGE
in Bangkok, Thailand

Designed by Supermachine Studio
Photo© Wison Tungthunya

The Bangkok University Lounge conceived by local studio Supermachine is a multi-story facility geared towards enhancing student learning experience. The design team has put together their talent and creativity to remodel the 600-square-meter student lounge to accommodate a variety of student activities, and to encourage creativity and progressive interactive teaching.

Within the vibrant, dynamic space with irregular shapes, bold forms, and playful elements, a eye-popping color palette of bright pink, yellow, and lime, creates a playful learning environment and encourages flexible experimentation. The transparent materials, the neon pixel walls, the light-reflecting surfaces and the peculiar perspectives all add to this eccentric, unconventional design.

On the lower floor of the lounge, the "Reading Cave" displays a fascinating wall of wooden ribs, in front of which the "big sofa" is situated with pixel units that can be formed in different configurations. The upper level has been formed for more dynamic activities and consists of two huts: a shocking polka dotted pink karaoke house and a wooden room for small events. Play areas surround the two huts, filled with re-invented items such as a pool, ping pong tables, a giant panda bear room and a pole dancing corner. An intriguing network of holes throughout the space provides visual connection and highlights the quirkiness and energy of the lounge.

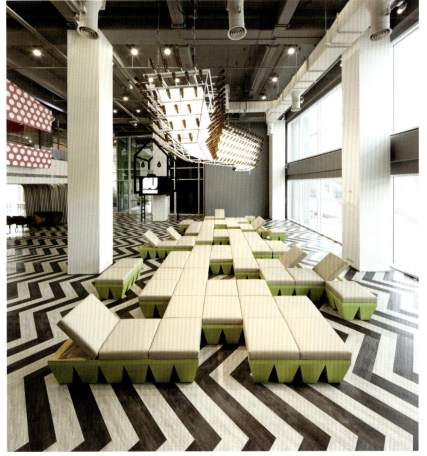

VAN ALEN BOOKS
in New York, USA

• •

Designed by LOT-EK
Photo© Danny Bright

LOT-EK was commissioned by the Van Alen Institute to conceive and design Van Alen Books, a new architecture and design bookstore and public reading room located at the organization's headquarters in Manhattan's Flatiron District. Motivated by an urgent need for spaces where architecture books can be discovered and discussed, Van Alen Books is beyond its role as a destination bookstore.

This dynamic space offers a place where books can be read and debated through a curatorial program exploring the past and future of architectural publishing. Inviting the public to linger and browse, the store features a 14-foot-tall seating platform crafted from a stack of 70 recycled doors, which ascend to create an amphitheater overlooking 22nd Street through glazed storefront windows. Sourced from Build It Green! NYC, a non-profit supplier of salvaged building materials, the solid wood doors form a triangular installation evoking the steps of Times Square's TKTS booth, an iconic project originated from Van Alen Institute's 1999 design competition.

This highly visible space is New York City's only book emporium and gathering place devoted singularly to architecture and design publications, and an open platform to discuss the future of architecture books.

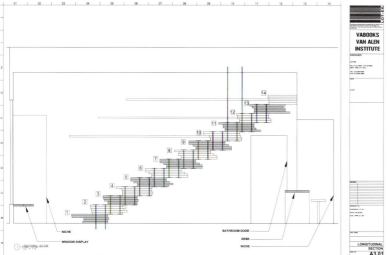

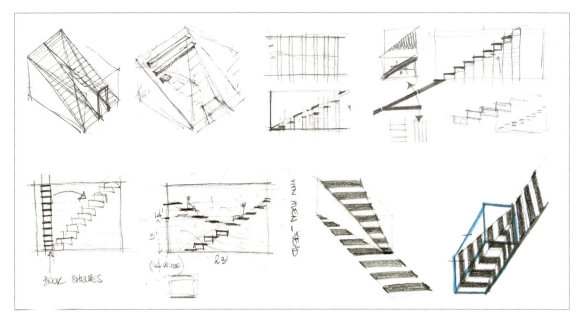

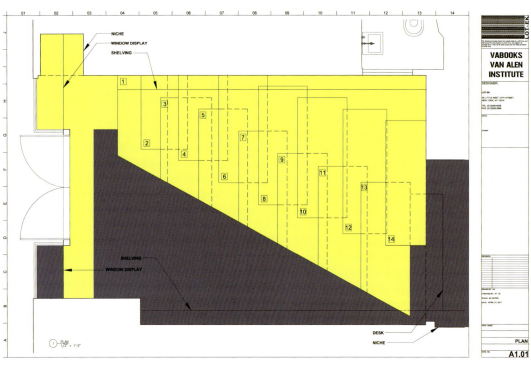

ING BANK SLASKI CORPORATE DEPARTMENT
in Warsaw, Poland

Designed by Robert Majkut Design
Photo© OLO Studio

Polish architect Robert Majkut has completed a dynamic bank office for ING Bank in Warsaw, Poland. In order to keep up with the pace of technological progress, Majkut created a fluent interior enveloped with undulating walls.

The architect used several strategies that merge the design and the CI of ING office to emphasize the bank's functionality. The internal walls in curves are coated in orange and white creating smooth surfaces throughout the space, encircling the reception, meeting rooms, corridors and other administration areas. The LED lighting set inside the glazed walls provide good illumination for the interior. The functional rooms are set with furniture in corporate colors: orange and white. The office design using beautiful curves and lively colors allow visitors to feel the vibrant pulse of the bank.

SPAINALIGHT
in Minato-ku, Tokyo, Japan

Designed by Stone Designs
Photo© Stone Designs

Madrid-based design studio Stone Designs was commissioned by ICEX (the Spanish Institute for Foreign Trade) to design this vibrant exhibition for Tokyo Designer's Week 2011, which was held at the Spanish Embassy in Tokyo. As an introduction to the Spainalight, the Embassy also commissioned a documentary about the influence of light in Spanish designs, "Spain, Light in the Creative Process". This design has won Stone Designs the Grand-Prix Award in 2012, and the documentary won the silver Laus 2012.

In the documentary, three Spanish artists from the world of architecture (Antonio Jiménez Torrecillas), industrial design (Joan Gaspar) and fine art (Daniel Canogar), also representing three Spanish cities were interviewed about their works and the way that light was used as a starting point in their various projects. In wanting to reflect the Spanish elements, Stone Designs showed us a world of innovation and contrasts, as well as a melting pot of cultures. This vibrant design features various excellent Spanish designs under bright beams of light within frames embellished with orange shadows to symbolize how light has influenced our creation.

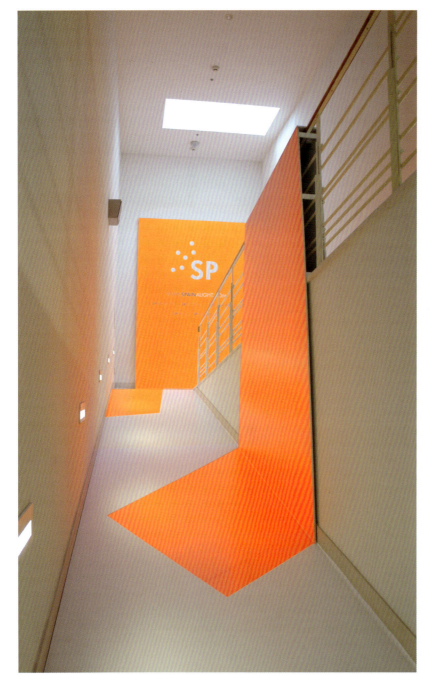

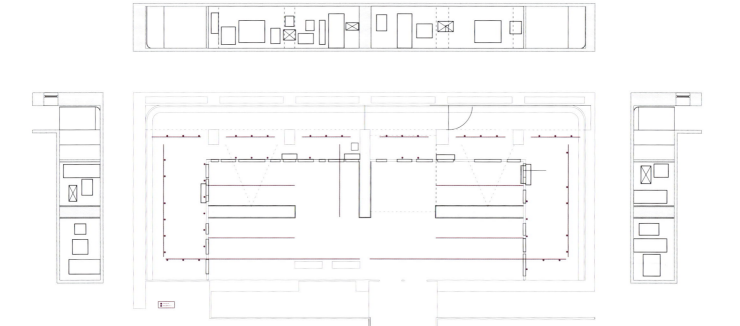

BAR OPPENHEIMER
in New York, USA

Artist: Tobias Rehberger
Photo© Matthias Cianfrani/ Courtesy Pilar Corrias, London

"The way I look at it is like a suitcase," Rehberger said, "I'm going to be in New York for a bit so I'm able to pack up my favorite bar and take it with me. And because I'm there for the art fair, the bar has to come dressed as a work of art."

German artist Tobias Rehberger created a temporary replica of his favorite Frankfurt bar at Hôtel Americano, a place where artists meet to discuss, argue, and pursue ideas. Functioning as both an installation and a working bar, it remained in place from 11 May until 14 July, 2013.

New York Bar Oppenheimer had exactly the same size and proportions of the original bar. It contained the same furniture and details, from the lighting fixtures to the tall radiators. Unlike the original, Rehberger decorated every surface of the replica bar with black and white stripes, which zigzag in every direction and are interspersed with flashes of red and orange. The patterns are based on the concept of "dazzle camouflage", a tactic employed during World War I to make it difficult for soldiers to pinpoint a target.

PULSATE
in London, UK

Designed by Lily Jencks & Nathanael Dorent
Photo© Hufton + Crow

Architects Nathanael Dorent and Lily Jencks have created a pop-up installation on Primrose Hill using Marazzi's SistemN ceramic tiles. There are two ideas within the installation: one is about perception—how one perceives distances, and shapes and makes sense of this environment. The other is about how to display an object for sale: the designers wanted the space to be more than just a shop laying out products and they look at commercial transactions as something more creative.

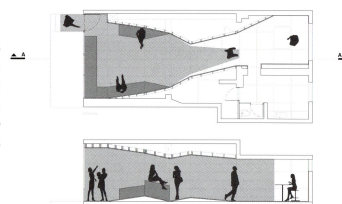

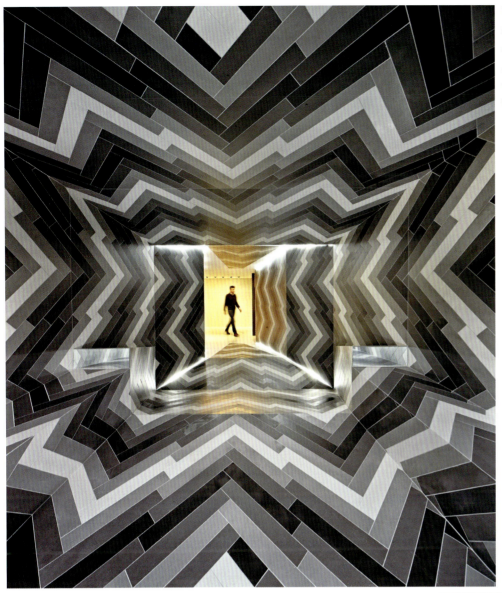

The immersive space that was created is shown from various points of views. We can see how the tiles that are covering walls, floor and ceiling create a singular environment that reflects in different ways the surrounding's lightings and colors.

Inspired by Op Art and Gestalt psychology, Pulsate creates a sense of forced perspective that will help draw people into the space. The pattern that is continuous on the floor, walls, ceiling, and furniture, disrupts how your eyes and mind make sense of the space, similar to an op-art painting. Jencks and Dorent decided to use one system of tiles in one size and four colors. Based on a simple herringbone pattern, they've applied it onto a sloped three-dimensional environment, to offer a unique experience for visitors as well as something eye-popping visible from the street. The pattern goes from dark to light, and then to dark in a gradient, like a pulsating wave. To achieve this showroom, the pattern and the supporting structure are tightly interrelated.

SAATCHI & SAATCHI AGENCY
in Bangkok, Thailand

Designed by Supermachine Studio
Photo© Wison Tungthunya

Supermachine was commissioned by Saatchi & Saatchi, Thailand to redesign their Bangkok office into an innovative workplace, a space "that inspires, genuinely fun to come everyday, and that does not take itself too seriously."

The agency located at a dated building in the Sindhorn Tower, Bangkok, has a 400-square-meter space. In order to furnish the tight space with a tight budget, the design team developed bold ideas—an unexpected design that leave much of the space open, featuring strong visual elements. The space has been re-arranged and divided into two functioning zones: a creative area and an administration one.

The reception desk is on wheels and resembles a big white bus that doubles as a moving bar counter. Bicycles in the creative area work as legs of a large conference table that is fully mobile, while a large wall is covered with small, white "wood pixels" that are made of wood recycled from the agency's previous office. With this wall, Supermachine covered the original red marble wall and saved costs, which also created a visual link to the Saatchi & Saatchi team's past.

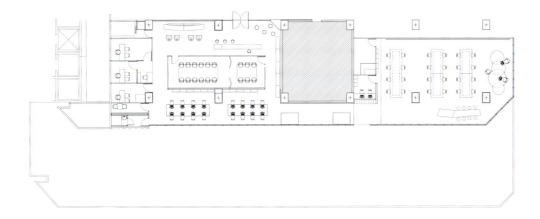

There is a monster wall that features a 20-meter-long lizard who has become the agency's new mascot. Its skin is embellished with current works and inspirational items, and its jaw works as a bookshelf.

With the visual theme reoccurring in the shape of a racetrack or stadium, this agency space is redecorated with bright colors and inspirational decorations, creating a playful and relaxing workplace.

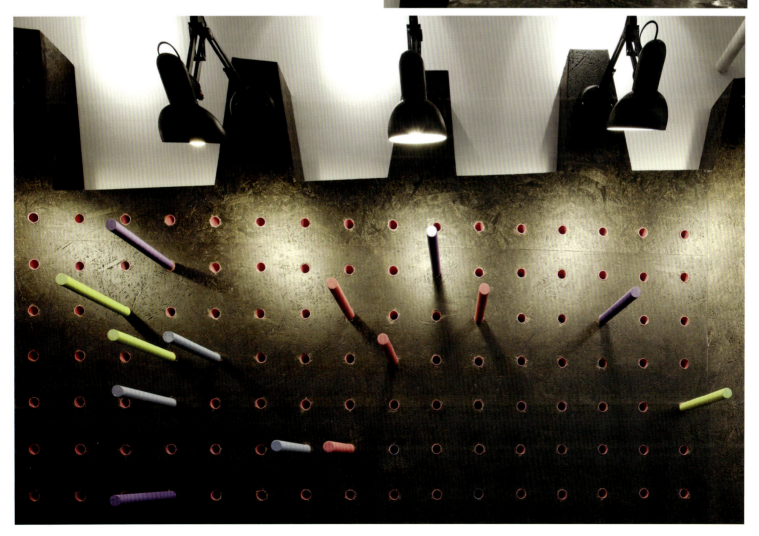

YOUNG AT ART MUSEUM
in Florida, USA

Designed by Architecture Is Fun
Photo© Doug Snower Photography, Emma Exley

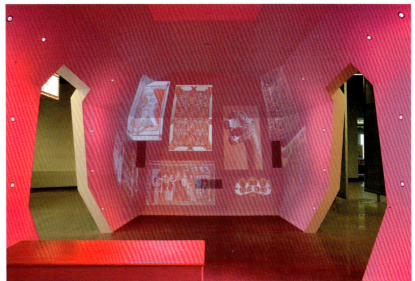

Young at Art Museum takes a sophisticated design approach to bridging the gap between an adult art museum and a children's museum. As an art museum for children, it features an exhibit space rich in branded environments, art installations, and art-making opportunities. Throughout the museum there is beauty and the development of aesthetic study. Color enhances each environment with layers of meaning and methods. In galleries, color is used symbolically to define and articulate connections to art, history, culture, nature, and wonder.

ARTSCAPES is designed for discovering the continuum of art history and one's place within it. It features the architecturally significant "Cave". As the first object visitors see, it serves as a metaphor, meeting place, orientation theatre, and art-making space. Its column-free structure is faceted and clad with super white, matte surfacing, which contributes to its mysterious nature. The "Cave" is a powerful portal of projected imagery and flashing colors. Selecting "museum white" for it was an archetypal decision reflecting the modernism prevalent in South Florida. Ideologically, the white form is a cool, modern counterpoint to ancient art. Demonstrating that this is a cave of today, inside 5,000 years of art history flash through a 4-D "flipbook": colors, light, media, and music.

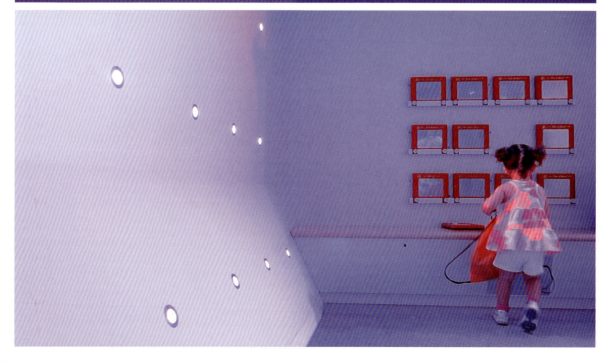

 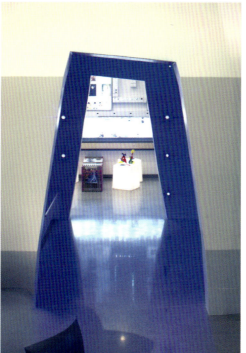 

As the very first museum experience, the "Cave" brands the paradigm-shift of learning about art to using art for learning. Young artists make their marks analogous to the first cave paintings and by doing so become part of the journey of art history that flashes on the screen. Visitors explore mark-making as they come to understand art's capabilities to communicate. A cave panel boasts an image of a Paleolithic Lascaux cave painting. Prehistoric painters dug minerals and iron oxide from the ground, forming them into crayon-like sticks or liquid pastes resembling paint. The mixing of pigments is found throughout art history, from cave painters to Rembrandt and beyond. Within the museum, colors move visitors through time and experience.

From the warmth of the "Cave", young artists next encounter "10,000 slides" where they can curate their own collections. Then they move to the Portrait Gallery, where portraiture is encouraged in an environment paying homage to nineteenth century art salons. The design is particularly referential to the elegance of Sir John Soane's Dulwich College Picture Gallery, a purpose-built space for viewing art. Soane's fearlessness about using strong color is employed within this children's gallery. "Dulwich-red" permeates the patterned wall coverings, tufted salon sofas, and vividly painted walls, focusing attention, layering views and creating atmosphere. Within this Portrait Gallery, color is the element that creates a branded realism with powerful art-making experiences.

From antiquity to the present day, color has been embedded with cultural meaning. The archeology gallery has a richness of color that looks back to the polychromatic colors found in classical architecture. In CULTURESCAPES, environments focus on contemporary global artists, whose art and color palettes are influenced by cultural traditions. Art-making, art installations, and color palettes align within the space, celebrating and forging understandings of our diverse world.

Within the museum's early childhood adventure WONDERSCAPES, inspiration comes from the classic story of *Alice in Wonderland*, adding shine, shimmer, high contrast, tactile and sensorial experience, all of which add vibrancy, color and artful delight to a world for toddlers and infants.

Art and color are a powerful force at the vibrant Young At Art Museum, a world of play and learning enhanced by aesthetic sensibilities.

EVOLUTION BAR
in Bucharest, Romania

Designed by Sebastian Barlica & Wanda Barlica
Photo© Ciprian Stoian, Serban Bonciocat

Located at the historical center of Bucharest known as Cafeneaua Veche ("The Old Café"), the eclectic Evolution Bar designed by Romanian designers Sebastian & Wanda Barlica is in contrast with the existing 18th century neo-gothic building, bringing a fresh and contemporary feel with a new interior.

Barlica blended the old building's historical values and the owner's demands and warmed up the two-level space with a glass HI-MAC bar top, interesting hose pipe chandeliers and a few other light touches. The space is arranged with a Mediterranean restaurant on the first floor and a night club in the basement that is designed with durable materials.

The basement initially used for storage is a brick vault with transverse arches, which made it quite challenging for the designer to transform this small space into a contemporary area for clubbing and nightlife entertainment. In order to achieve this purpose, Sebastian Barlica designed a floating U-shape bar counter in green and a custom designed honeycomb-like translucent modular for glassware suspended above the counter within the Evolution Bar. The bar area is lit with suspended neon lights and furnished with colorful furnishings such as stools and couches, which create a dramatic change to the space. In this eclectic mix of an original brick vault and modern decoration details, the contemporary high-tech bar looks like an alien ship landed from nowhere.

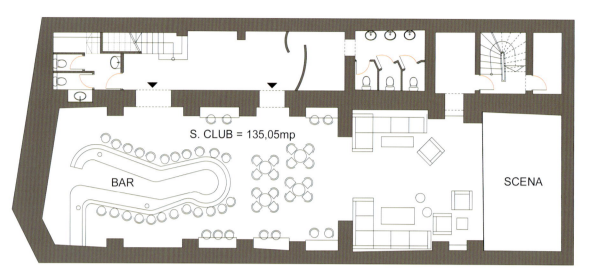

S. CLUB = 135,05mp

BAR

SCENA

PLAN SUBSOL

MARTIAN EMBASSY
in Sydney, Australia

• •

Designed by LAVA
Photo© Brett Boardman, Peter Murphy

International firm LAVA has designed the Martian Embassy for The Sydney Story Factory, a non-profit organization in Redfern, Sydney, in collaboration with Will O'Rourke and The Glue Society.

In wanting to take the visitor out of their ordinary surroundings and further stimulate their creativity and imagination, LAVA created an alien environment with a giant plywood installation and an amazing lighting system. The interior of the writing center consists of 1068 CNC-cut curvilinear plywood sections coated in Martian-green paint, which resemble a strange intergalactic fusion between a whale, a rocket and a time tunnel. The wooden ribs, which are assembled like puzzle pieces, use their shapes as ornament. The negative spaces between are used for shelves, benches, displays and storage to maximize the utilization of the structure.

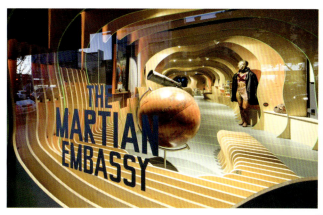

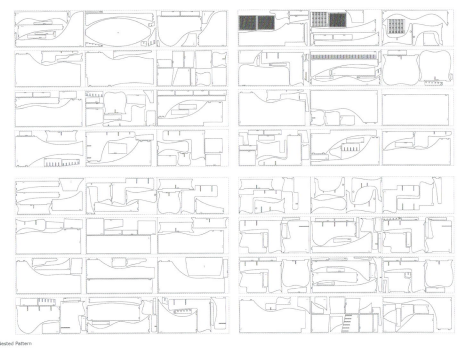

Nested Pattern

The entrance receives humanoid visitors and introduces them to the environment complete with lights and sound effects. Upon further exploring the alien environment, there is a red planet traveler's shop, where an array of Martian products can be purchased and classrooms are available for earthling volunteers to assist visiting students in creating and developing their stories.

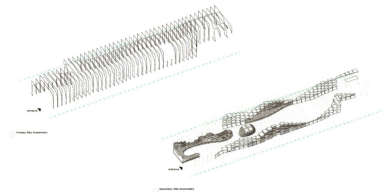

TOLEDO METRO STATION
in Naples, Italy

Designed by Oscar Tusquets Blanca

Photo© Peppe Avallone, Andrea Resimini, Luciano Romano, Giovanni Fasanaro y Oscar Tusquets

Napoli's metro station programs have been going on for some time with artists, designers and architects, including Alessandro Mendini, Anish Kapoor, Gae Aulenti Jannis Kounellis, Karim Rashid, Michelangelo Pistoletto and Sol LeWitt contributing. The Toledo Metro Station project by Spanish firm Oscar Tusquets Blanca is the thirteenth Art Station of the Naples Metro system.

Located under one of the main shopping streets in Naples, Oscar Tusquets designed the station with two metro entrances. The Toledo station is based on a more than 40 meters deep cavern and themed around "water" and "light". Oscar Tusquets Blanca has teamed up with two artists, William Kentridge and Bob Wilson to complete this wonderful art design that houses two levels. The upper level capped with natural stones seems to be excavated in the rock. The floors and walls of the lower space are covered in varying shades of blue bisazza mosaics by the architect, offering a feeling of being underwater with its ocean ambiance. In addition, the designers have also adopted a dynamic LED lighting system along with the color palette for the space, creating the dizzying effect of a starry night.

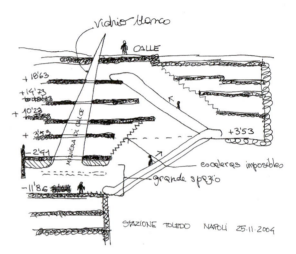

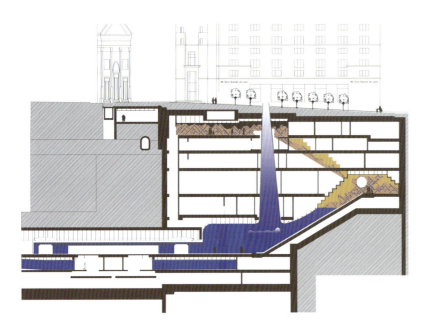

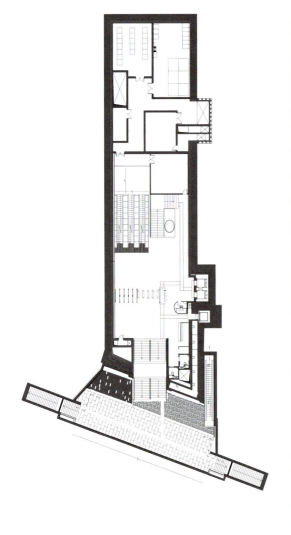

Functional Colors

ST-EXUPÉRY SPORTS AND LEISURE CENTER
in Saint-cloud, France

Designed by KOZ ARCHITECTES
Photo© Stephen Lucas

This childishly simple, cubist building for festive celebration and young people evokes happy memories of children's toys. With its cheerfulness and non-conformist style, the building contrasts strongly with the urban development zone in which it's located, behind a new block of private apartments and next to neo-Haussmannian offices and a day-nursery in a similar style.

The block is a vertical piling of activity spaces (a gymnasium, climbing walls, the leisure centre, and various functional areas) wrapped in a ribbon of concrete providing unity to the whole. Concrete is a natural choice as it highlights the building's sculptural appearance while satisfying different spacial, insulation and aesthetic requirements.

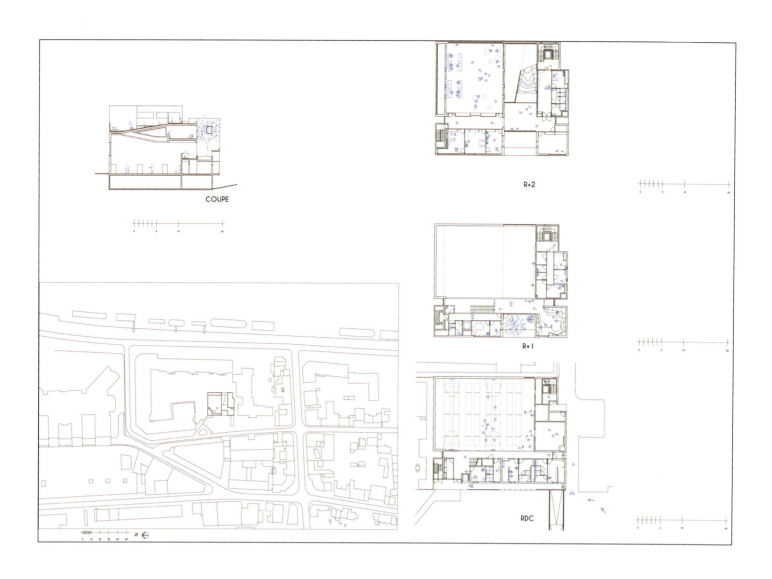

COUPE

R+2

R+1

RDC

The openings in the roof and the glass façade bring maximum natural light in to limit electrical consumption. A pure colour scheme supports the building very openly and assertively, with a wide palette ranging from red, green, yellow, to pink and orange, covering the façade in wide stripes. Inside, the same colors are systematically repeated, just like an oversized graffiti.

The colour coding also helps visitors locate from the outside the areas inside, a means of spatial orientation for young children, at the same time adding a sense of street culture to the environment for those who crawl on what has dubbed "the coolest indoor climbing wall" in France, or practice on the pop fencing rows below!

21 CAKE HEADQUARTERS
in Beijing, China

Designed by People's Architecture Office
Photo© People's Architecture Office

Beijing-based design firm People's Architecture Office has completed the new 21 Cake Headquarters for the popular gourmet pastry franchise in Chaoyang District, Beijing, China. The two-level light-grey office topped with a large skylight is bathed in vibrant hues with a vivid design language. The interior enveloped with white surfaces provides a backdrop to laminated panes of primary colors, red, blue and yellow, which visually overlap to create rainbow-like effects inside. These laminated panes are positioned to divide the office zones providing functional areas that are illuminated by natural light from the skylight and artificial light in the interior. The white furniture with unconventional shapes can fit into one another like puzzle pieces, allowing for flexibility in space and function. All the rich flavors of vibrant tones inside the space create a dramatic effect in such an inspiring workplace.

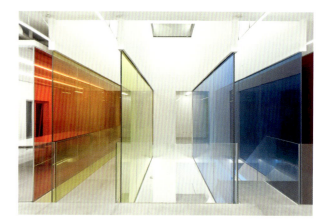

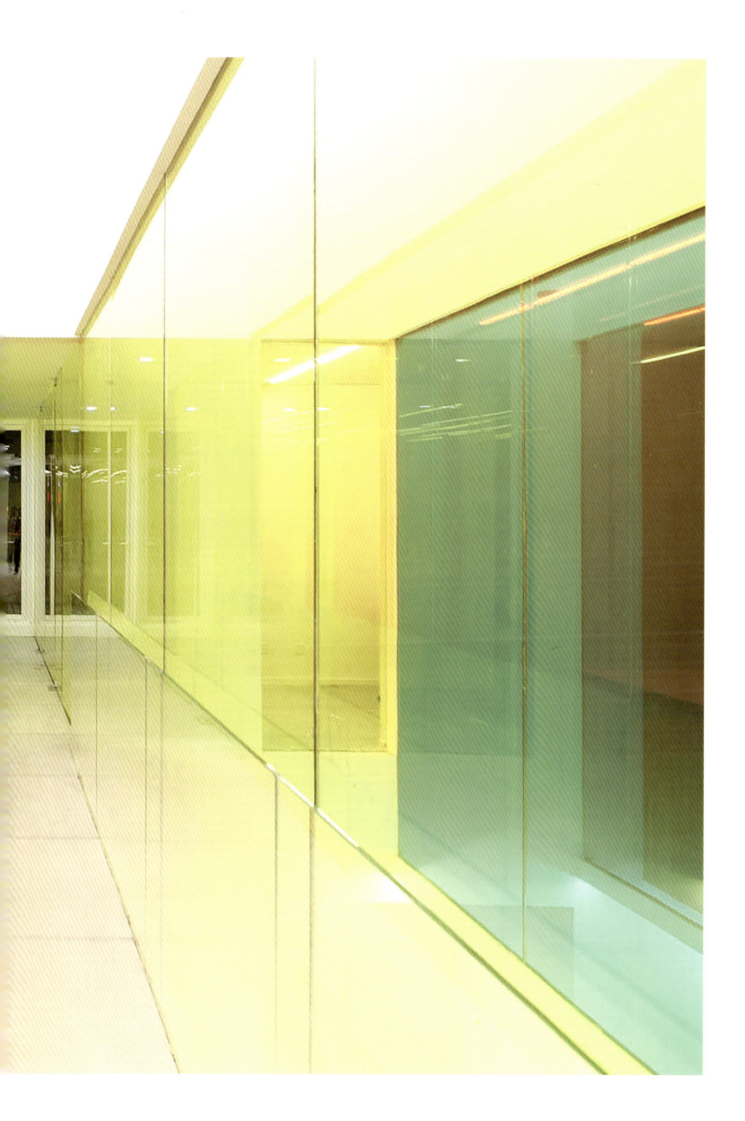

CHILDCARE FACILITIES
in Boulay, France

Designed by Paul Le Quernec
Photo© Paul Le Quernec & 11h45

Strasbourg-based architect Paul Le Quernec has concieved and completed the childcare facilities in Boulay and a micro-nursery in Piblange to explore the contextual fluidity of buildings by giving a smooth façade and functional areas.

To cut down on vehicle circulation, the building is accessed through a one-way lane which limits parking and decreases the risk of accidents involving pedestrians. The drop-off area is located next to the sidewalk where the entrance is set back from the road and from oncoming traffic, so parents don't have to cross the street.

The building was constructed using traditional methods and materials, even though the structures are designed with atypical shapes. The façades are made of insulating clay bricks, covered by 20cm-thick re-enforced mineral wool, which are then treated with plaster and painted like a pointillist canvas.

The undulating exterior follows the interior circulation of the building which is organized around a protected central space. At the core of the nursery, a circus tent-like wooden structure expands to a three-meter-wide vaulted ceiling, made of polycarbonate to allow light to filter into the facility. On the north side of the building, the mechanical spaces (boiler room, electrical room, etc.) are painted in bright red like a fire engine and the administrative areas are coated with grass-green, while the south area reserved for children is yellow-colored and the playground is shielded from sun or rain with an extended roof.

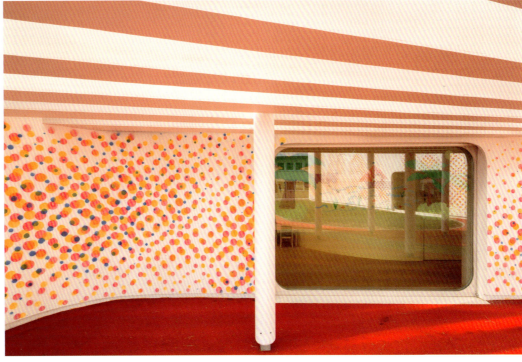

The load-bearing internal walls are made of reinforced concrete which support the laminated wooden beams. These are curved and were mass-produced to decrease the manufacturing cost. A single-layer, damp-proof membrane covers the roof, while perforated plaster boards protect the ceiling, also improving the acoustical comfort of the space. The under-floor heating system is finished in linoleum which matches the color of the internal solvent-free ecological paints. The doors and windows are made of wood to meet BBC (low energy-use building) energy performance standards.

AMSTELVEEN COLLEGE

in Amstelveen, the Netherlands

Designed by DMV architects
Photo© John Lewis Marshall

Amstelveen College in the suburb of Amsterdam, the Netherlands has been transformed into an innovative and practical new building by DMV architects from inside out.

The four-storey building for Amstelveen College has been designed to be a creative and arresting edifice with unconventional volumes. The building with an open terrace is separated into seven independent diminutive departments, each with an outdoor activity area and an entry point that leads to a central area. To emphasize different functions of the seven departments, each volume of the building is coated in a unique color against a black backdrop.

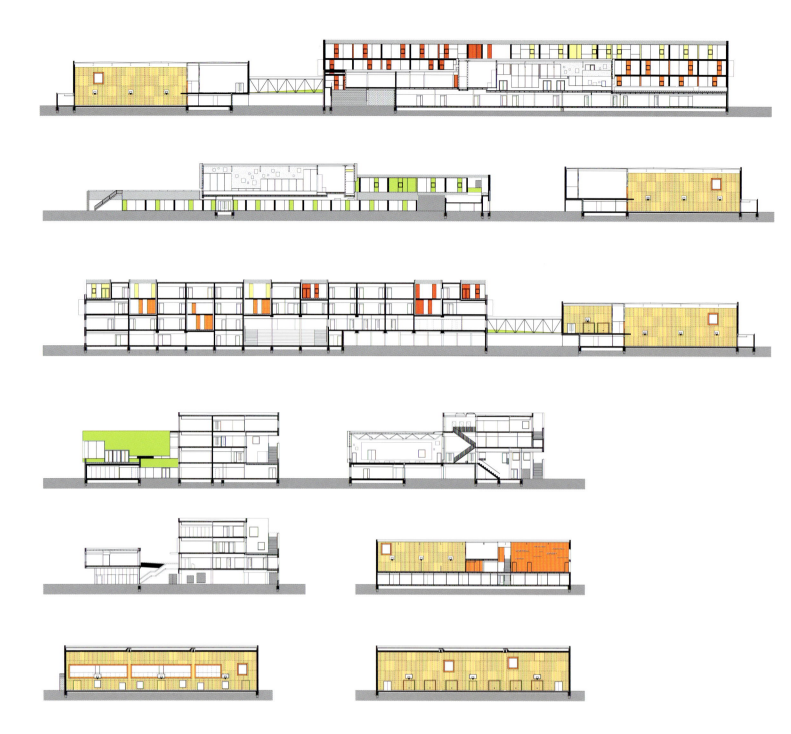

Each department, with almost two hundred students, meets each other in a large stair hall with several skylights to allow light to filter into the lively interior capped with natural green. Functional areas such as class rooms and offices are scattered around the central point on both floors. On the first floor, there are labs for biology, chemistry and physics as well as art and music classrooms completed with large French windows. Accessible by an over-line corridor, there is an indoor double-height sports hall with different colored stripes in a concealed volume. The sports hall, which is lit with artificial lights, was designed to be an environmental program that takes on a balanced ventilation system inside, as well as a solar heating system on the roof.

The aesthetic volumes for the college not only provide an enclosed environment for students and also introduce a significant building type to the site.

AGORA THEATER
in Lelystad, the Netherlands

Designed by UNStudio
Photo© Christian Richters, Iwan Baan, Hans Luiken

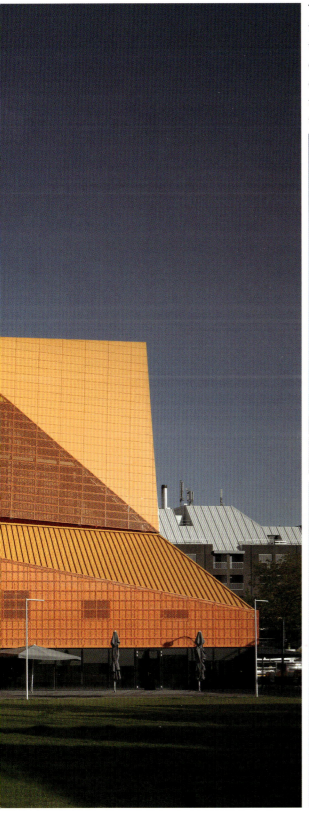

The Agora Theater is an extremely colorful, determinedly upbeat place. It responds to the ongoing mission of reviving and recovering the post-war Dutch new towns, by focusing on the original function of a theater: that of creating a world of artifice and enchantment. Both inside and outside walls are faceted to reconstruct the kaleidoscopic experience of the world of stage. In the Agora Theater drama and performance are not restricted to the stage and to the evening, but are extended to the urban experience and to the daytime.

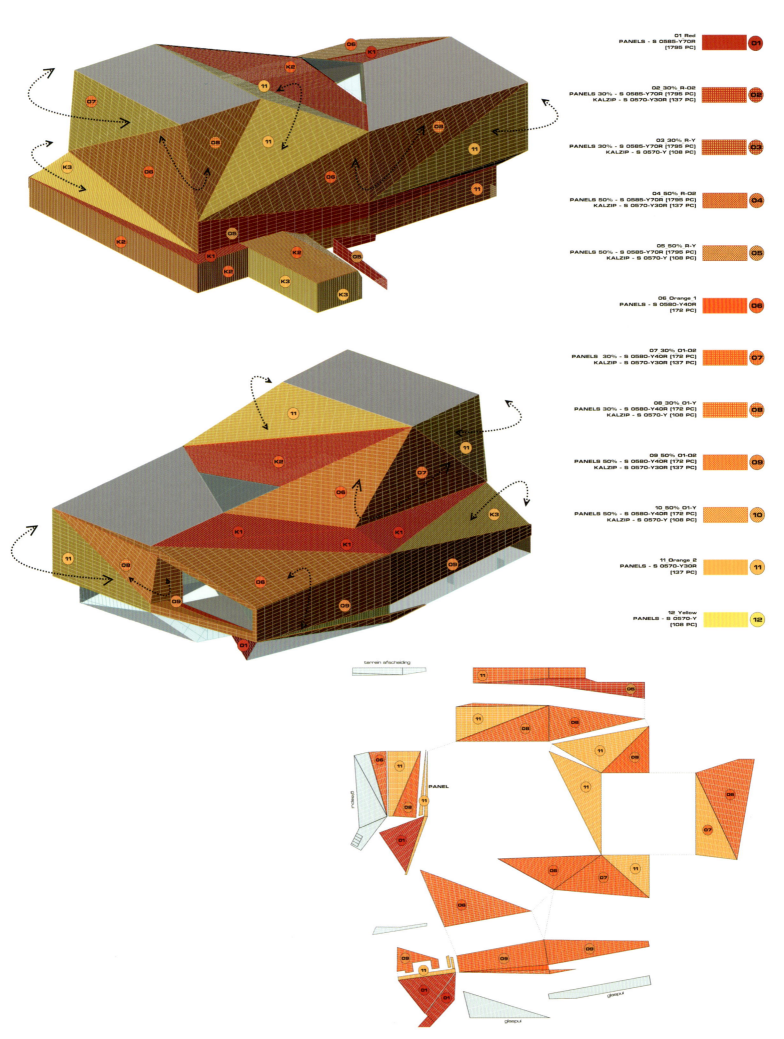

01 Red
PANELS - S 0585-Y70R
[1795 PC]
01

02 30% R-02
PANELS 30% - S 0585-Y70R [1795 PC]
KALZIP - S 0570-Y30R [137 PC]
02

03 30% R-Y
PANELS 30% - S 0585-Y70R [1795 PC]
KALZIP - S 0570-Y [108 PC]
03

04 50% R-02
PANELS 50% - S 0585-Y70R [1795 PC]
KALZIP - S 0570-Y30R [137 PC]
04

05 50% R-Y
PANELS 50% - S 0585-Y70R [1795 PC]
KALZIP - S 0570-Y [108 PC]
05

06 Orange 1
PANELS - S 0580-Y40R
[172 PC]
06

07 30% 01-02
PANELS 30% - S 0580-Y40R [172 PC]
KALZIP - S 0570-Y30R [137 PC]
07

08 30% 01-Y
PANELS 30% - S 0580-Y40R [172 PC]
KALZIP - S 0570-Y [108 PC]
08

09 50% 01-02
PANELS 50% - S 0580-Y40R [172 PC]
KALZIP - S 0570-Y30R [137 PC]
09

10 50% 01-Y
PANELS 50% - S 0580-Y40R [172 PC]
KALZIP - S 0570-Y [108 PC]
10

11 Orange 2
PANELS - S 0570-Y30R
[137 PC]
11

12 Yellow
PANELS - S 0570-Y
[108 PC]
12

terrein afscheiding

PANEL

glaspui

glaspui

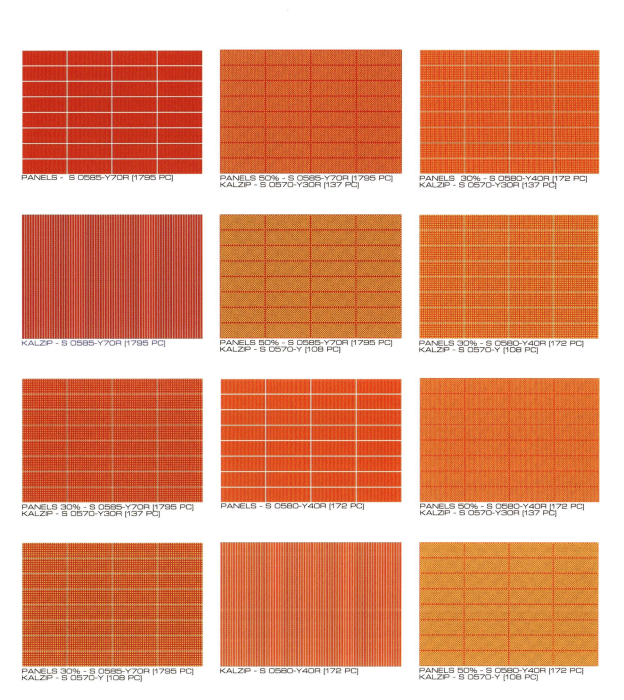

PANELS - S 0585-Y70R [1795 PC]

PANELS 50% - S 0585-Y70R [1795 PC]
KALZIP - S 0570-Y30R [137 PC]

PANELS 30% - S 0580-Y40R [172 PC]
KALZIP - S 0570-Y30R [137 PC]

KALZIP - S 0585-Y70R [1795 PC]

PANELS 50% - S 0585-Y70R [1795 PC]
KALZIP - S 0570-Y [108 PC]

PANELS 30% - S 0580-Y40R [172 PC]
KALZIP - S 0570-Y [108 PC]

PANELS 30% - S 0585-Y70R [1795 PC]
KALZIP - S 0570-Y30R [137 PC]

PANELS - S 0580-Y40R [172 PC]

PANELS 50% - S 0580-Y40R [172 PC]
KALZIP - S 0570-Y30R [137 PC]

PANELS 30% - S 0585-Y70R [1795 PC]
KALZIP - S 0570-Y [108 PC]

KALZIP - S 0580-Y40R [172 PC]

PANELS 50% - S 0580-Y40R [172 PC]
KALZIP - S 0570-Y [108 PC]

First Floor Plan

Second Floor Plan

Third Floor Plan

The typology of the theater is fascinating in itself, but Principal Architect and Co-founder of UNStudio Ben van Berkel, who has a special interest in how buildings communicate with people, aimed to explore the performance element of the theater and of architecture in general far beyond its conventional function. As he stated: "The product of architecture can at least partly be understood as an endless live performance. As the architectural project transforms, becomes abstracted, concentrated and expanded, becomes diverse and ever more scaleless, all of this happens in interaction with a massive, live audience. In Agora Theater, we can feel that the specificity of architecture is not itself contained in any aspect of the object. The true nature of architecture is found in the interaction between the architect, the object and the public. The generative, proliferating, unfolding effect of the architectural project continues beyond its development in the design studio, in its subsequent public use."

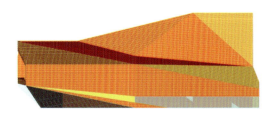

The envelope is generated in part by the necessity to place the two auditoriums as far apart from each other as possible for acoustic reasons. Thus, a large and a smaller theatrical spaces, a stage tower, several interlinked and separate foyers, numerous dressing rooms, multifunctional rooms, a café and a restaurant are all brought together within one volume that protrudes dramatically in various directions. This faceted envelope also results in a silhouette; the raised technical block containing the stage machinery, which could otherwise have been a visual obstacle in the town, is now smoothly incorporated. All of the facades have sharp angles and jutting planes, which are covered by steel plates and glass, often layered, in shades of yellow and orange. These protrusions afford places where the spectacle of display is continued off-stage and the roles of performers and viewers may be reversed. The artists' foyer, for instance, is above the entrance, enabling the artists to watch the audience approaching the theater from a large, inclined window.

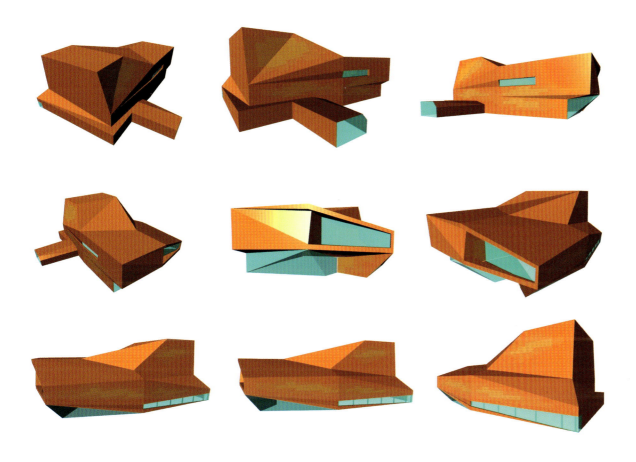

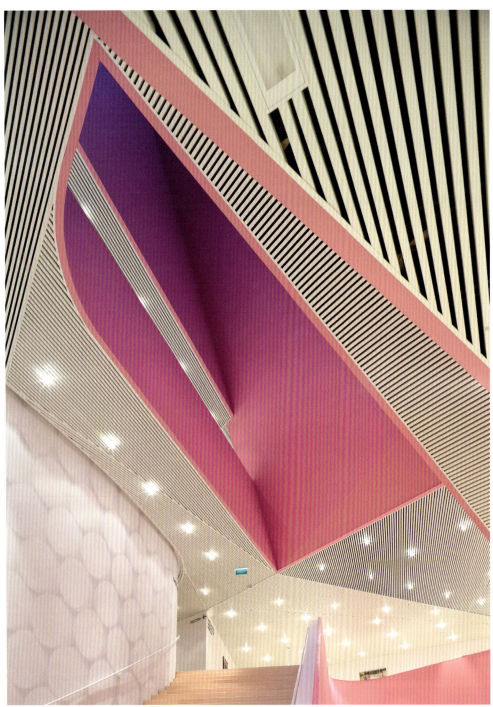

Inside, the colorfulness of the outside increases in intensity; a handrail executes as a snaking pink ribbon cascades down the main staircase, winds itself all around the void at the center of the large, open foyer space on the first floor and then extends up the wall towards the roof, optically changing color all the while from violet, crimson and cherry to almost white. The main theater is all in red. Unusually for a town of this size, the stage is very big, enabling the staging of large, international productions. The intimate dimensions of the auditorium itself are emphasized by the horse-shoe shaped balcony and by the vibrant forms and shades of the acoustic paneling.

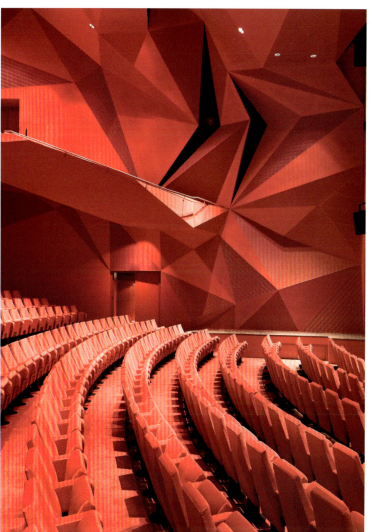

PAJOL KINDERGARTEN
in Paris, France

Designed by Palatre & Leclere Architects
Photo© Luc Boegly

This four-classroom Pajol kindergarten fuses rainbow colors with joy into the community. Parisian architecture office Palatre & Leclère has restored and reimagined the 1940s building, yet leaving the basic feel of the structure unchanged.

The front courtyard is designed as an urban symbol of the identity of an optimistic kindergarten. It unfolds on three levels, creating a playful environment for children. The façade is carved on the ground floor to the yard.

In Pajol Kindergarten, the designers used color boldly both inside and out. They gave a variety of shapes and forms to the furnishings and the walls. They also used a variety of textures, from tile and glass to rubber and wood in the play areas, rest areas and even in the bathrooms.

"We realized that the challenge was to make it functional and pleasant, reorganizing the space and opening on the courtyard outside, and then we thought of exploiting the existing gable walls. The rainbow became the driving force behind the project, heralding a time of good weather after the rain. Legend has it that at the foot of a rainbow is a treasure. The treasure here may be the new building, and the children who are the future. Education of children is fundamental and significant to our society. We wanted to bring hope to them, to the future."

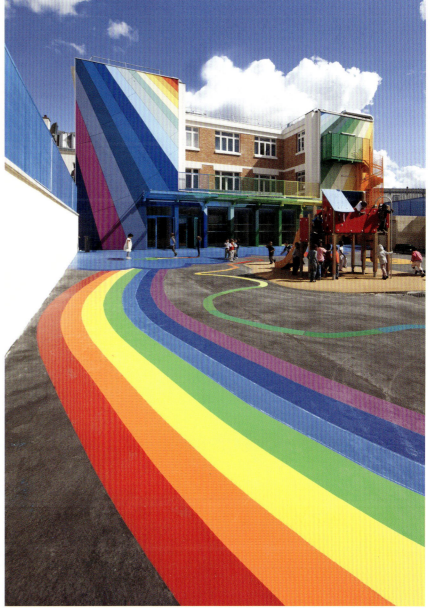

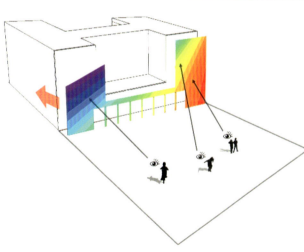

FITZROY HIGH SCHOOL
in Victoria, Australia

Designed by McBride Charles Ryan
Photo© John Gollings

MCR's design provides for the additional 225 students and 12 staff across three levels according to the school's expansion plan, interfacing with the existing 1960s school building. The model unit of the design is a space for between 40 to 60 students. Following a "team teaching" approach, the spaces are configured to allow for a flexible distribution of use, accommodating activities ranging from large "chalk and talk" lecture-style presentations to medium-scale seminar groupings to individual private study. This is achieved by a floor plan with an undulating perimeter, allowing for optimum supervision to occur within a variety of discrete spaces.

The undulating perimeter was constructed from double brick with a deep cavity, allowing the building's skin to perform structurally, thereby reducing the need for additional framing or bracing. The exposure of the inner skin of brickwork (and the underside of slabs) maximizes the building's latent thermal stability, considerably reducing the need for additional climate control. The exterior walls are coated in deliciously undulating color stripes, to help the structure stand out and to be consistent with the vivid colors embellished in the interior. The color scheme has won the team the 2010 Grand Prix at the Dulux Color Awards and many more.

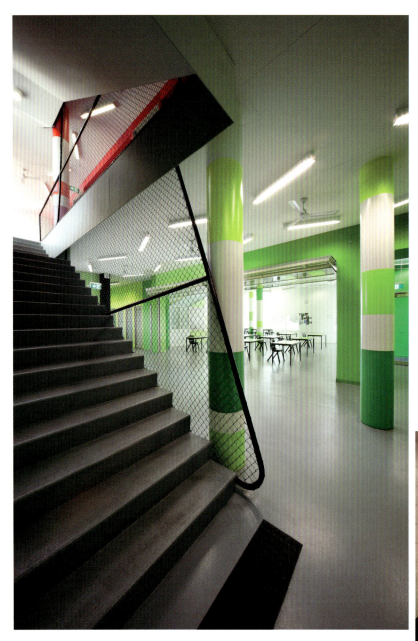

DECAMERON

in São Paulo, Brazil

Designed by Studio mk27
Photo© Pedro Vannucchi

"The project was aimed to be a design that can re-assemble
somewhere else. In designing Decameron, we used containers
to form the architecture, enabling mobility of the project."

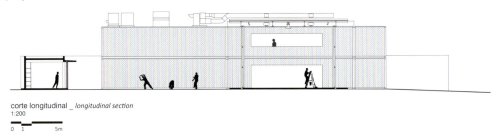

corte longitudinal _ *longitudinal section*
1:200

0 1   5m

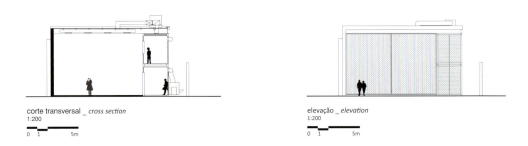

corte transversal _ *cross section*
1:200

0 1   5m

elevação _ *elevation*
1:200

0 1   5m

implantação _ siteplan
1:1250

0   5   25m

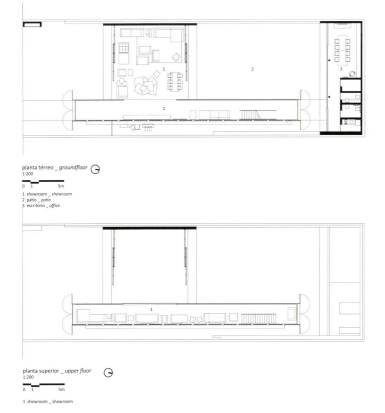

planta térreo _ groundfloor
1:200

0   1   5m

1 showroom _ showroom
2 pátio _ patio
3 escritório _ office

planta superior _ upper floor
1:200

0   1   5m

1 showroom _ showroom

This retail store project Decameron has won Brazilian architects Marcio Kogan and Mariana Simas the world's best shopping building award at the world architecture festival. The showroom of Decameron furniture store is located at a rented site and designed with a limited budget. To achieve the economic construction, the project worked with the premise of a light occupation of the lot, basically done with industrial elements, which could easily be assembled. The displays of Decameron are placed within a stack of two containers which are oriented perpendicular to the main street, assisted with a new adjoining structure which is characterized by two sliding doors, one as the entrance and the store-front, the other opening to a beach-like patio with pebbled ground. The bold and vibrant colors painted on interior part of the containers are revealed when the large and translucent sliding doors of the new structure, are unfolded during the store's operation hours.

Products are shown in line along the walls of the narrow hallways in the containers, limited by the inherent dimensions of the units, which cross the main volume to introduce a movement as they are in the process of being transported by a truck. An arrangement of furniture within the adjoining, clear-span structure allows visitors to experience the products. Further back is a courtyard garden with planted palm trees and a pebbled ground, which creates a serene atmosphere to buffer the back office from the common areas. The large glass wall of the office ensures furniture designers an access to the sales scene. Two edges of the design process come into contact through the inner patio as other opposing strengths also meet at this small project: the intensity of urban life and a small nature retreat; the power of the containers and the lightness of the metallic structure; and finally the linearity of the tunnels and the cubic volume.

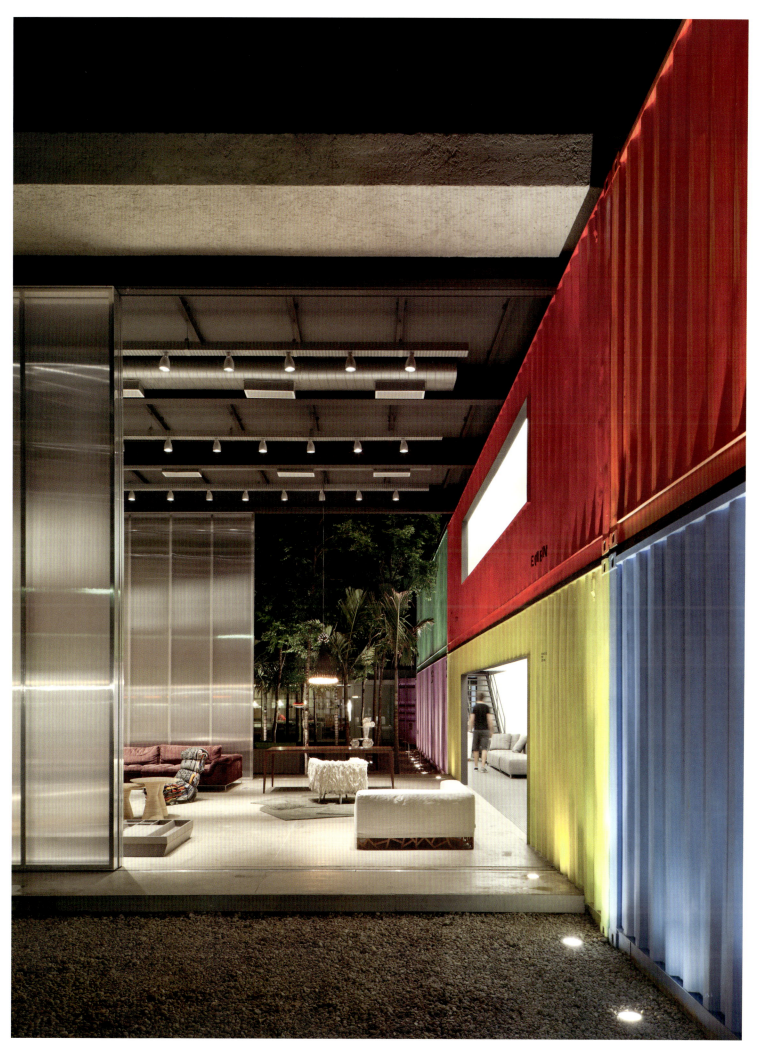

THE WAHACA SOUTHBANK EXPERIMENT
in London, UK

Designed by Softroom Ltd
Photo© Joseph Burns

The Wahaca Southbank Experiment is a new two-storey temporary restaurant installation, constructed from eight recycled shipping containers that have been "washed up" on to the outdoor terrace of the Queen Elizabeth Hall, at the Southbank Center by the Thames River in London.

The idea for using the shipping containers was developed not only to remind visitors to the restaurant of the working history of this part of the Thames river, but also for more practical reasons as their limited height allowed Softroom to be able to fit two floors into the volume of a single-storey space.

Situated against the heavy concrete backdrop of the Queen Elizabeth Hall, each container is painted in one of four vibrant colors ranging from deep turquoise to straw yellow, providing a colorful contrast to the restaurant's gray surroundings. The color choices make reference to both the painted façades of typical street scenes in Mexico, and the color compositions often seen in container ships and ports.

One of the top floor containers has been cantilevered out over the restaurant's ramped entrance to create a canopy above the first floor. On the upper level, this cantilevering heightens views from the upstairs bar out over the river towards Westminster.

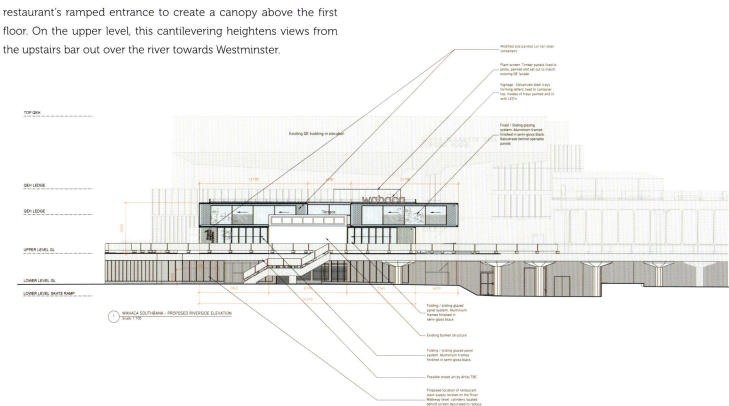

Modified and painted cor-ten steel containers

Plant screen. Timber panels fixed to posts, painted and set out to match existing QE facade

Signage. Galvanized steel trays forming letters fixed to container top. Insides of trays painted and lit with LED's

Fixed / Sliding glazing system. Aluminium frames finished in semi-gloss Black. Balustrade behind openable panels

Existing QE building in elevation

TOP QEH

QEH LEDGE

QEH LEDGE

UPPER LEVEL GL

LOWER LEVEL GL

LOWER LEVEL SKATE RAMP

wahaca

Terrace

Folding / sliding glazed panel system. Aluminium frames finished in semi-gloss black

Existing bunker structure

Folding / sliding glazed panel system. Aluminium frames finished in semi-gloss black

Possible street art by Artist TBC

Proposed location of restaurant plant supply located on the River Walkway level cylinders located behind screen decorated to reduce visibility.

1 WAHACA SOUTHBANK - PROPOSED RIVERSIDE ELEVATION
Scale: 1:100

PLANNING

VERIFY ALL DIMENSIONS ON SITE
DO NOT SCALE

REVISION   DATE   NOTES
             06.01.12   ISSUED FOR PLANNING

SOFTROOM 341 OXFORD STREET LONDON W1C 2JE
T +44 (0)20 7400 0864 F +44 (0)20 7400 0863
SOFTROOM@SOFTROOM.COM WWW.SOFTROOM.COM

FOR WAHACA

▷ SOFTROOM

PROJECT WAHACA SOUTH BANK
TITLE   PROPOSED RIVERSIDE ELEVATION
STATUS   PLANNING

DATE   SCALE   PROJECT NO DRAWING NO REVISION
01.12 1:200@A3   1119   (PL)07   -
       1:100@A1

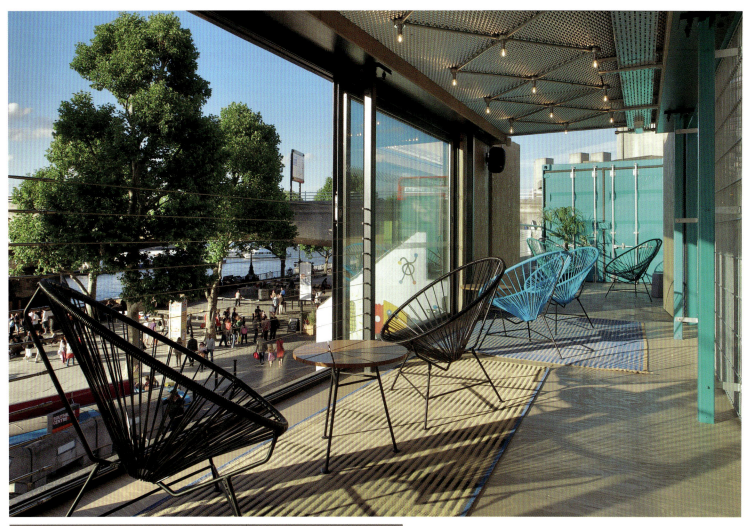

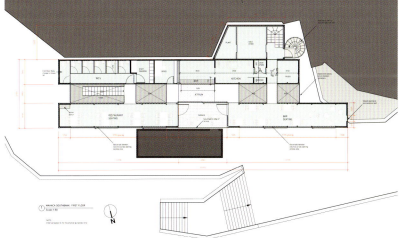

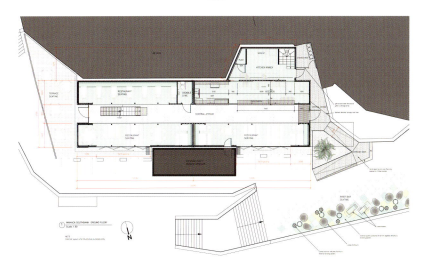

Inside the restaurant, the front and back containers are connected via a glazed link, which not only houses the stairway connecting the two floors, but also helps to flood the space with natural light. Each of the containers has then been given its own character with a mix of bespoke, new and reclaimed furniture along with distinct lighting designs. Outside, there is a wide variety of areas in which to sit, from the booth seats, built in to the raised timber deck around the building, to the second floor terrace bar, to the street bar overlooking Queen's Walk.

BERCHTESGADEN YOUTH HOSTEL
in Bavaria, Germany

Designed by LAVA
Photo© Robert Pupeter

The Berchtesgaden Youth Hostel "Haus Untersberg" in Bavaria, Germany, which was built in the 1930s, has been redesigned by the Australian/German architecture firm LAVA. Based on recent trends in the hospitality industry, LAVA placed the same importance on simplicity, individuality, and authenticity as other hotel typologies in this youth hostel.

The modernization and re-design of the interior targeting families has been completed within the existing plan. To create a stronger sense of community, the old building was remodeled into a hostel with well-arranged zones allowing for more open spaces on the ground and mezzanine level. The designers also personalized the bedrooms with built-in storages, creating an integrated environment which avoids the typical barracks style facilities. These built-in zones link the internal parts of the building with the surrounding landscape.

DG

2. OG

1. OG

EG

UG

Lager

Familienzimmer

Galeriezimmer

Familienzimmer

Balkonzimmer

Balkonzimmer

Terrasse

Terrassenzimmer

Snowlounge

Lager

Elektroraum

Legende

Terrassenzimmer in ehemaligem Gemeinschaftsbereich

Balkonzimmer bei Bestandsterrassen

Familienzimmer

Galeriezimmer, zweigeschossig unter Dach

Snowlounge

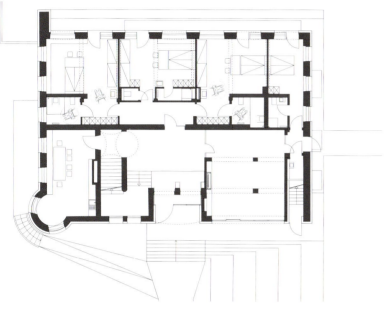

Bestand   *Möblierungskonzept LAVA*

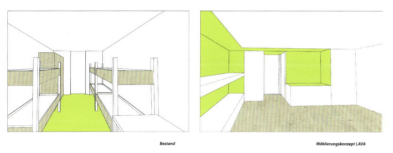

LAVA director Tobias Wallisser said, "The blending, overlapping and interlinking of different spheres influences society today. This constantly evolving process is what gives LAVA's Hostel Berchtesgaden form and shape by providing flexible but highly recognizable spaces. A special quality of comfort is achieved by integrating simple and efficient technology".

In order to achieve a sustainable building, the new volume is fitted with a low energy façade, internal underfloor heating and a biomass pellet system. The cantilevered window boxes on the front façade act as seating, table areas and viewing platforms for relaxation. The entrance foyer is painted with colorful strips where each one represents the national flag of each European country. The bright color motif contrasts with the locally sourced and crafted materials. The re-arranging of the interior zones and the modernization of the building have given the existing structure a brand new identity and transform the building into a relaxing destination for families.

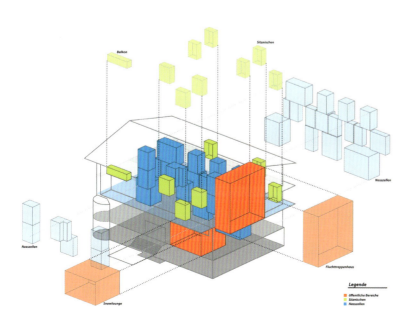

TDM5: GRAFICA ITALIANA
in Milan, Italy

Designed by Fabio Novembre
Photo© Pasquale Formisano

The exhibition designed by Fabio Novembre in Triennale Design Museum is located at the Palazzo dell'Arte-Triennale, which has hosted international and temporary exhibitions since 1923. The fifth exhibition TDM5: Grafica Italiana showcased twentieth century Italian graphic art and reflected changes in Italian culture and society. Triennale Design Museum has been engaging with the promotion and enhancement of Italian creativity, especially Italian design.

Upon entering the museum building, designed by architect Michele De Lucchi, a bamboo footbridge suspended above the central staircase links the design area and other parts of the building. Guided by color coding through a labyrinthine universe, visitors would find themselves in an area structured by tall white walls, resembling blank pages of an open book, each with differently colored markings. Along the route, the book fills up with stories, documents and objects, starting with futuristic photography but also inheriting traditions of previous centuries.

With the purpose of "helping the public understand what role Italian graphic artists have played in the history of the country, and how they have contributed to shaping its economic, social and cultural climate", Novembre used Greek mythology (the nine Muses and the labyrinth,) to divide the exhibition space into nine zones, representing the nine main aspects of graphic art: letters, books, magazines, culture and politics, advertising, packaging, visual identity, signs, films and videos.

"We decided to begin with the blank pages of a book, studying their physical structure and filling them with life in motion, setting their contents in various sections spread along a careful path. Sections deriving from that Platonic solid associated with the Earth, the cube, to cut it up and breaking it down to trace a labyrinth, like some new Daedalus, conjuring up an initiatory as well as celebratory experience," explained Fabio Novembre.

BANGKOK UNIVERSITY BRANDING UNIT
in Bangkok, Thailand

Designed by Supermachine Studio
Photo© Pitupong Chaowakul

Bangkok University Branding Unit for the University has been redesigned by Bangkok-based design firm Supermachine Studio. This Branding Unit, a former childcare house, was transformed into a creative office that stimulates people to express themselves. With a limited budget, the designer simply refreshed the interior zones with vivid colors. The interior and the furniture in the staircase hall are painted in pink, while the kitchen is embellished with blue objects. New walls and new-painted doors and windows have been installed in the 400-square-meter house with three colors: rose, blue and yellow. The designers simply used the bright colors to signify and divide the unit, which have been splashed all over the space finally.

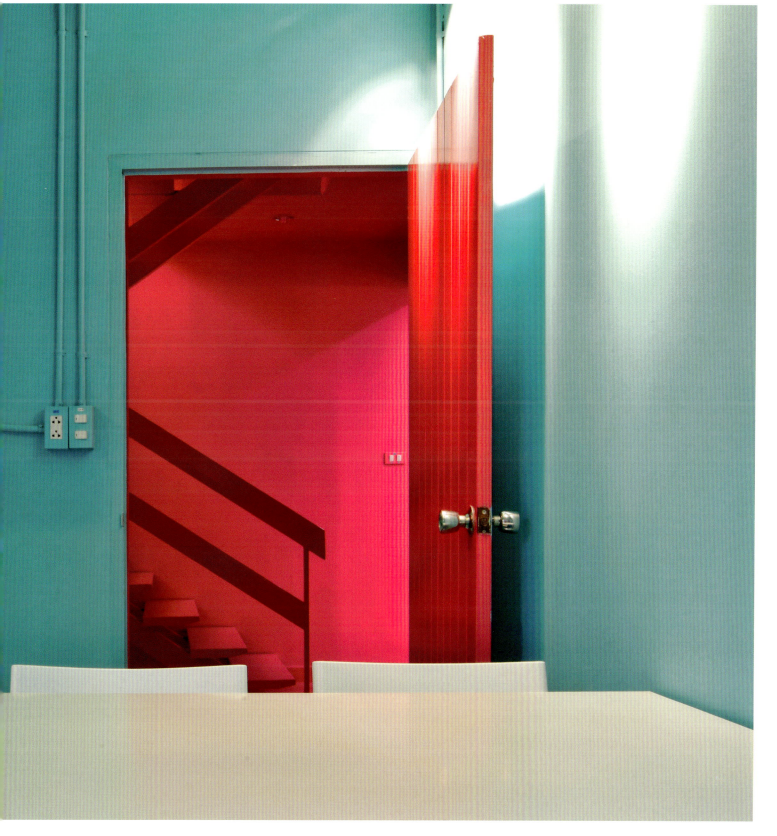

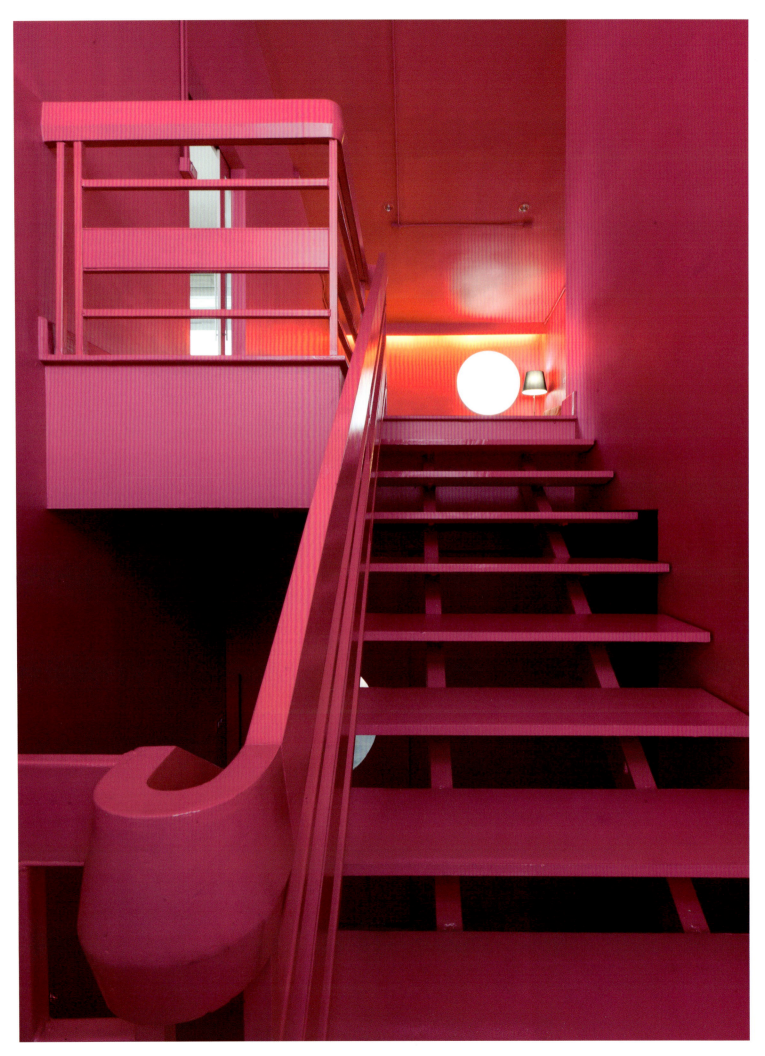

YANDEX SAINT PETERSBURG OFFICE II
in Saint Petersburg, Russia

Designed by za bor architects
Photo© Peter Zaytsev

This is the eighteenth design by Russian studio Za Bor Architects for the technology company Yandex, which is currently the largest search engine in Russia. Located in St. Petersburg's Benois Business Center, the design integrates a series of contrasting unusual objects throughout the interior of the building—architects Arseniy Borisenko and Peter Zaytsev wanted to give guests the impression of being "inside the Yandex search service."

The new Yandex St. Petersburg office is designed to be a computer-desktop-like space, with colorful pixelated backgrounds and huge icons. The architects organized the interior zones along a 200-meter-long corridor, where screens and shelves take on shapes of a music play button, cursor arrows, the "@" symbol and even a Pacman logo. Administration Areas, such as conference halls and meeting rooms framed by ribbon-like shapes and colored curtains, are scattered along the entire work-space, while leisure areas such as a gym and café lounges are also added to this internet company. A large bulbous clock is set in the corridor with a printing station concealed behind. The reception desk resembles a text box, where a computer user inputs their username or password, giving the entire office a virtual, game-like feel.

FARMACIA SANTA CRUZ

in Santa Cruz de Tenerife, Spain

Designed by Marketing Jazz
Photo© Ikuo Maruyama

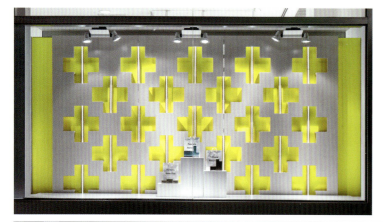

Spanish studio Marketing Jazz has won the first prize at the 42nd International Store Design Awards by Santa Cruz Pharmacy project in 2012. The 300-square-meter pharmacy located in Santa Cruz de Tenerife, features designated shopping zones for easy navigation. Market Jazz integrated the pharmacy concept within the entire store with periodic oversized tables, against the medicine shelves as background.

Taking customers' shopping experience into consideration, the designers set the pharmacy in an open layout to ensure an effortless flow.

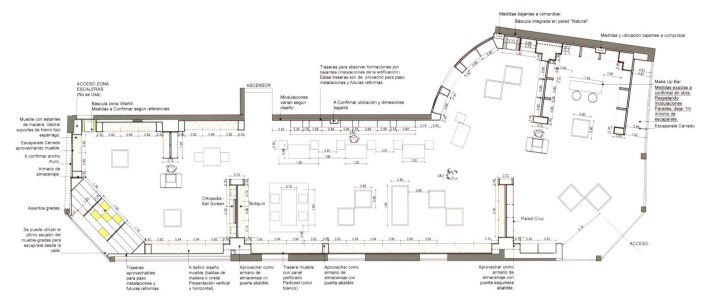

In the middle of the store, dimmable, recessed fluorescent downlights help fill the store with soft, ambient light. Lights are angled down from the four-meter-high ceiling, tracking discreetly the products and accenting the display. Lighting design in this chemistry-lab-like space serves as a guide, helping customers explore the store and easily find desired products and services. A special waiting area in the first floor allows the elderly or handicapped to relax while waiting for their service.

SENZOKU GAKUEN COLLEGE OF MUSIC "THE BLACK HALL"
in Kanagawa, Japan

Designed by TERADA DESIGN ARCHITECTS
Photo© Yuki Omori

Tokyo-based design studio TERADA DESIGN has furnished the new rock & pop music course of the music college in Kawasaki, Kanagawa, Japan with bright colors, signage and wayfinding systems. The "The Black Hall" has more than 6,000 square meters of floor area. It houses concealed zones including recording studios, classrooms and practice rooms. In order to stimulate the creativity and inspiration of students, TERADA DESIGN simply used colors to divide the zones, as well as oversized colorful numbers to navigate in the entire interior according to varied requirements.

4F

3F

2F

1F

FABRICVILLE
in Gothenburg, Sweden

Designed by Electric Dreams
Photo© Electric Dream

"Fabricville" in Gothenburg, Sweden designed by Electric Dreams is a creative and funny company headquarters, a three-floor office for Fabric Retail, Weekday and Monki, an interesting mix of fashion designers, buyers, construction managers, and PR people. The inspiration behind this design was the idea that a busy company headquarters is very much like a little village—it gathers many types of occupations, each with different spatial requirements, and many different activities are going on at different times.

This three-story office was designed to house 150 employees within a little village in a 1,500-square-meter space. The village were based on traditional Swedish wooden cottages, combining rural dwellings of traditional build with a modern environment. The long narrow corridors became a busy village street, with workshop buildings for clothing designers, office buildings for marketing staff, and bright-colored cottages for conference rooms. The main street is lined with laser-cut MDF hedges on each side, and the canteen is the green park in the middle. Each floor has a different color scheme to match the brand identity.

MCCANN-ERICKSON RIGA OFFICE
in Riga, Latvia

Designed by Open Ad
Photo© Maris lagzdins, Didzis Grodze

Latvia-quartered design firm Open Ad has completed the creative McCann-Erickson office in Riga, Latvia, whose interior is warmly lit and stylish, with great splashes of colors and a "Tree of Knowledge" for a library.

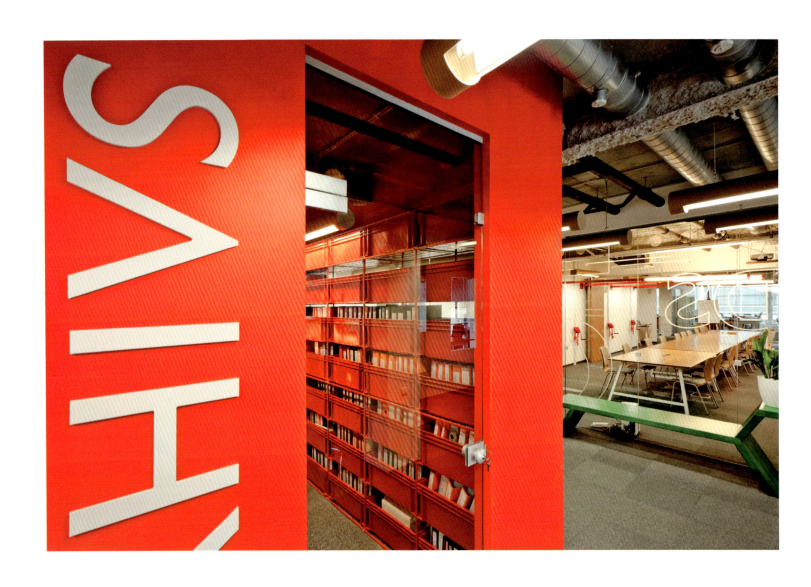

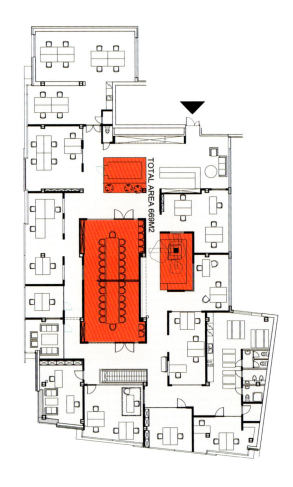

TOTAL AREA 669M2

The design team has employed recycled materials such as panels from left-over timber products, and household and office appliances in this 640-square-meter space. The interior, which is embellished with white-painted walls and raw furniture in vivid colors, is well-organized within the functional floor plan. The designers also recycled high diameter pasteboard tubes to help create lighting for the office. Being a low budget project, Open Ad worked with recycled simple materials to develop a "trash style", creating a relaxing and inspiring atmosphere for the artistic interior.

RED TOWN OFFICE
in Shanghai, China

Designed by Taranta Creations

Shanghai-based Taranta Creations has transformed a former metal factory into an unconventional workspace, for their new office in Red Town Sculpture Park in Shanghai, China.

An existing diagonal steel structure stood in the way of creating a two-storey office within the 120-square-meter space, as the designers had originally desired. The distance between the structure and the ceiling was too small to fit a traditional office layout between; thus the design team built a floor just above the structure.

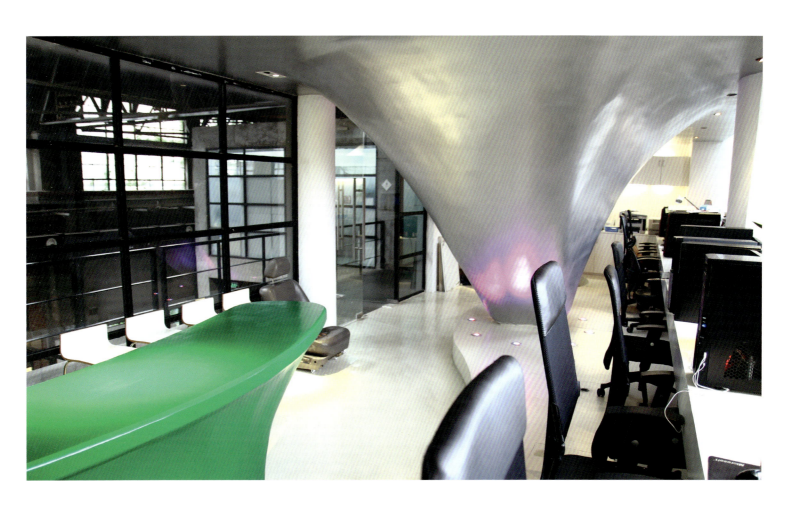

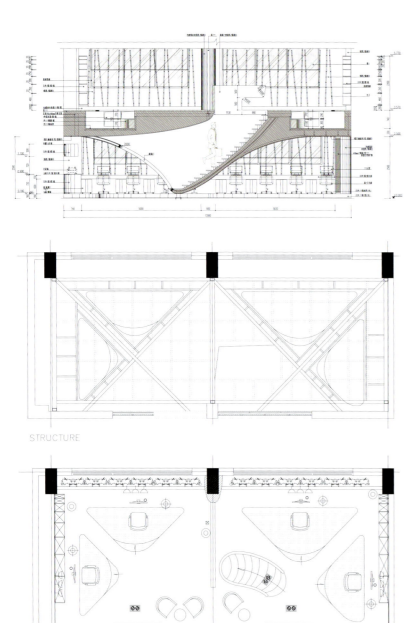

STRUCTURE

LAYOUT TOP FLOOR

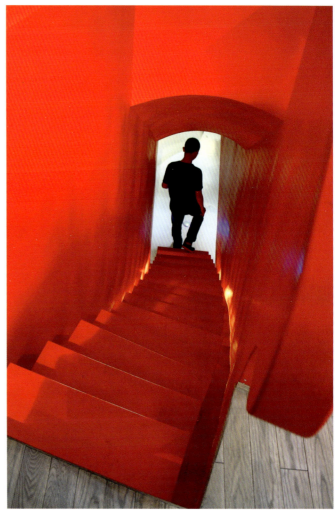

Below, the lower level has a normal layout with workstations along a window, while a green table for activities is placed behind a staircase, painted red inside and silver outside. On the second level, accessible by the staircase, four working stations are depressed in one continuous desk that doubles up as the floor.

"The large 'work floor' invites designers to use the open space for thinking, sketching, meeting, drafting, modeling, sitting and relaxing", said the design team.

YANDEX KAZAN OFFICE
in Kazan, Russia

Designed by za bor architects
Photo© Peter Zaytsev

Russian Internet company Yandex has an office in Kazan, which is situated at Suvar Plaza business center, designed by local design studio Za Bor Architects. The creative office design that revolves around a central corridor is arranged within a 647-square-meter trapezoidal layout.

Yandex offices are well-known for unconventional zones and linear arrangements, which have also been brought in to this Kazan office. Za Bor Architects placed functional semi-closed rooms alongside the main corridor instead of concealing them within the office. These small rooms adopt various shapes, adorned with monochromic green walls inside, and white ones outside as well as different-colored furniture. Black wooden floors are used to give a contrast with the white interior walls, while the ceilings are sheeted with acoustic panels to ensure a comfortable workplace. In order to provide good illumination, the office is lit with oversized candlestick-like lights and table lamps that are hung down from the ceiling.

ISELECT

in Victoria, Australia

Designed by V Arc
Photo© Yvonne Qumi/YQ Photography

Australian design firm V Arc has completed an unconventional design for the Cheltenham-based iSelect team with a wowing effect.

The 4,800-square-meter site split across three levels, marries contemporary design practice with space planning. In order to design a vibrant office environment, V Arc designed the company into a family-like workplace.

Upon entering iSelect, there is an open area coated in the company's corporate colors, orange and white, with a round zone that encircles white furniture providing a relaxing meeting area. In wanting to make the call center stand out, the designers set oversized earphone-like lamps hanging dowm from the ceiling.

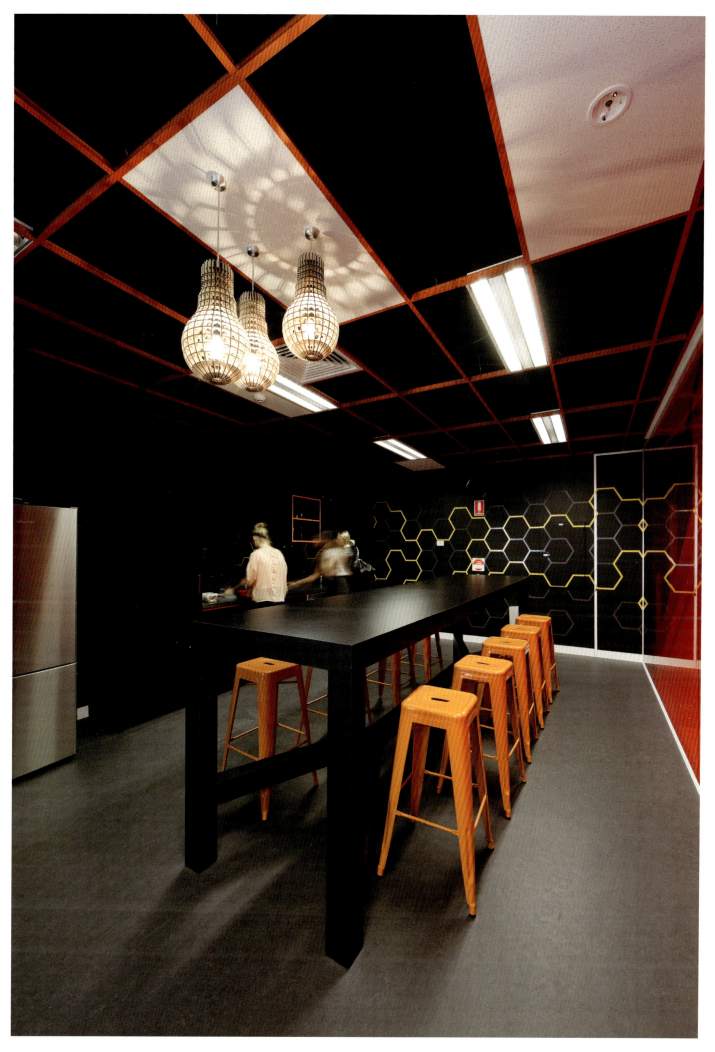

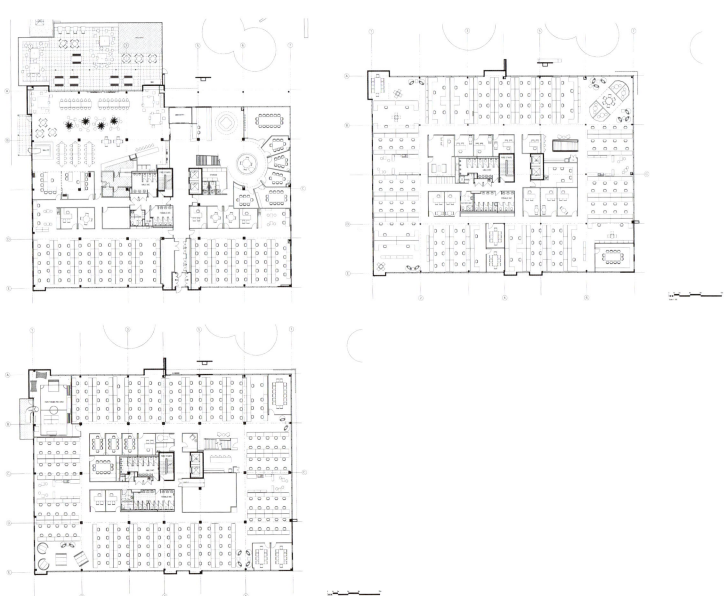

The interior is designed into administrative and relaxing areas. The administrative areas, such as meeting rooms are scattered round iSelect offices, while the relaxing areas include a café lounge, an indoor soccer pitch and iPod player-like lounges. An orange slide from the outside leads to a ball pool within the 300-square-meter café, which is the centre of the layout. V Arc also employed colored furnishings in these areas, in contrast with the white grounded space, creating a cozy atmosphere.

KALEIDOSCOPE INSTALLATION
in Tokyo, Japan

· ·

Designed by emmanuelle moureaux architecture + design
Photo© Hidehiko Nagaishi

Japan-based French architect and designer Emmanuelle Moureaux designed an installation at CS Design Center in Tokyo, which displays 1,100 colors in the same space. With a "kaleidoscope" theme, the exhibition focuses on one color at a time such as yellow, red, green, blue or black. Every month, the space displays a different color, changing hues like a kaleidoscope, which aims to rediscover ordinary colors in our life.

ATOMIC SPA | BOSCOLO MILANO
in Milan, Italy

Designed by Simone Micheli Architects
Photo© Jurgen Eheim

Italian architect Simone Micheli has completed the design of a wellness center at Boscolo Hotel in Milan, Italy. In wanting to create a breathtaking space, Micheli used various blue "bubbles" with a white backdrop within the futuristic world.

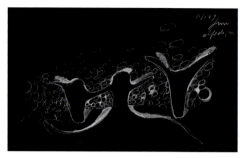

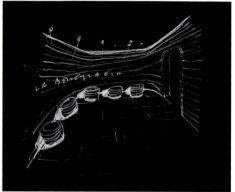

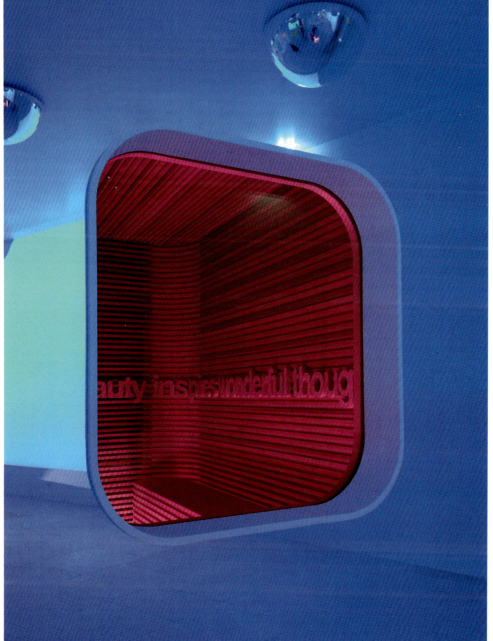

The architect divided the interior into administrative zones and relaxing areas including treatment cabins, saunas, and a large swimming pool, providing Turkish bath, showers and saunas. Upon entering the interior, a reception area with white furnishings welcomes visitors to explore this colorful undersea-like space that is embellished with various translucent bubbles in the ceilings. Accessible by a long and narrow corridor, which is scattered with treatment cabins on one side and features porthole-like display windows for products on the other side, there comes the central area of the Spa. At the heart of the wellness center, the shower areas are designed with big white tree structures that seem to hold up the whole space. The blue "bubbles" resemble raindrops hanging on the ceiling and the walls, ready to fall into the pool. The space goes with two circular skylights, providing iconoclastic illumination to the shower areas with vibrant colors and flavors.

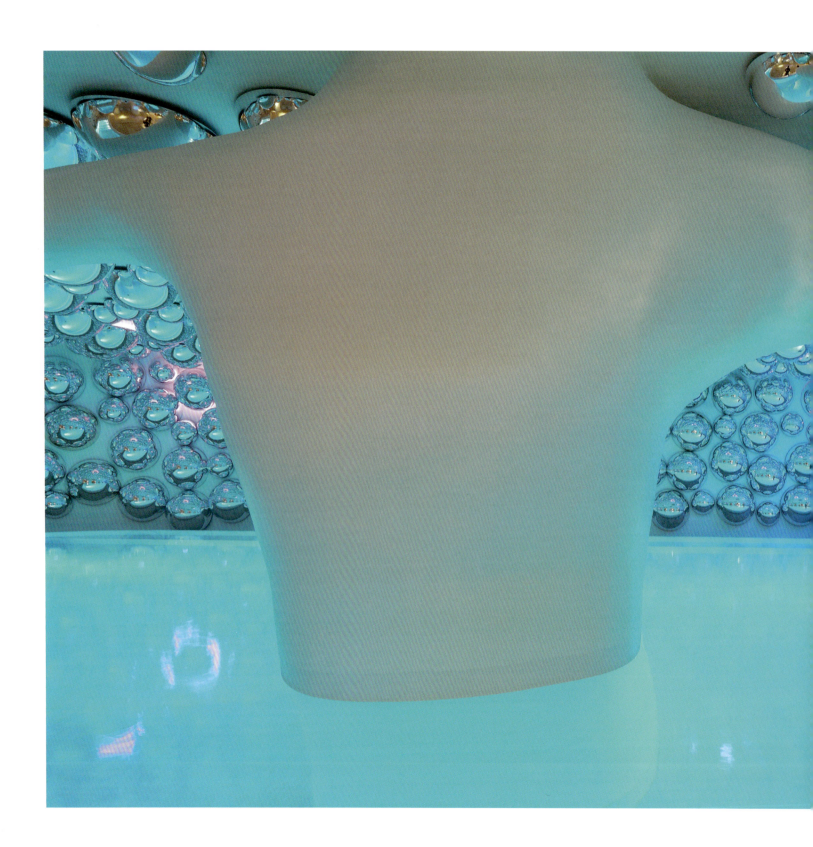

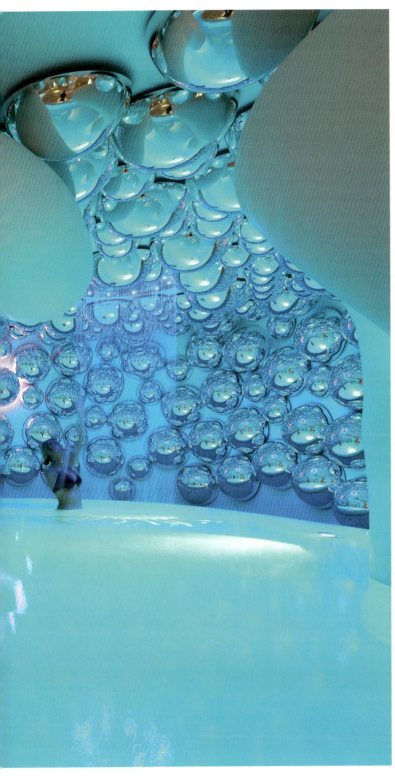

-Index-

ACKNOWLEDGEMENTS

We would like to thank all the designers and contributers who have been involved in the production of this book. Their significant contribution is indispensable in the compilation of this book. We would also like to express our gratitude to all the producers for their invaluable opinions and assistance throughout this project. And to the many others whose names are not credited but have made specific input in this book, we thank you for your continuous support.

FUTURE COOPERATIONS: If you wish to participate in SendPoints' future projects and publications, please send your website or portfolio to editor01@sendpoints.cn

429421